Africa's Billionaires

Forbes AFRICA

Africa's Billionaires

Inspirational stories from the continent's wealthiest people

CHRIS BISHOP

founding editor of *Forbes Africa*

PENGUIN BOOKS

Published by Penguin Books
an imprint of Penguin Random House South Africa (Pty) Ltd
Reg. No. 1953/000441/07
The Estuaries No. 4, Oxbow Crescent, Century Avenue, Century City, 7441
PO Box 1144, Cape Town, 8000, South Africa
www.penguinbooks.co.za

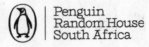

Penguin
Random House
South Africa

First published 2017
Reprinted in 2017 (twice)

3 5 7 9 10 8 6 4

Publication © Penguin Random House 2017
Text © Chris Bishop

Cover illustration: iStock by Getty

PUBLISHER: Marlene Fryer
MANAGING EDITOR: Ronel Richter-Herbert
PROOFREADER: Genevieve Adams
COVER DESIGNER: Sean Robertson
TEXT DESIGNER: Ryan Africa
TYPESETTER: Monique van den Berg

Set in 11.5 pt on 16 pt Minion

Printed by **novus print**, a Novus Holdings company

MIX
Paper from
responsible sources
FSC® C022948

Penguin Random House is committed to a sustainable future for
our business, our readers and our planet. This book is made
from Forest Stewardship Council ® certified paper.

ISBN 978 1 77609 121 8 (print)
ISBN 9 78 1 77609 122 5 (ePub)

Contents

To Tony and Sheila Bishop –
the shining people who inspired me to dream

Foreword

THE LIFE OF an entrepreneur can never be fully understood until you have experienced it yourself. There is a misplaced notion that entrepreneurship means freedom. On the contrary, the journey of an entrepreneur is, ironically, one of infinite bondage – the result of an inordinate desire to succeed. This journey is a maze of responsibilities, not only to your family, but to the families of the staff who work with you, and to the stakeholders who are related to your business. I know this path only too well – I have traversed it for the last 28 years since leaving the Indian Army.

While entrepreneurship is never easy in any place in the world, it has additional encumbrances in emerging markets. Over a lifetime, I have worked in almost every emerging economy, including but not limited to the former CIS countries (Commonwealth of Independent States, the association of Soviet states created by Russia in 1991), the Middle East, South and South East Asia, and Africa. It does not matter which geography, the path is littered with uncertainty and volatility that can test the resolve of even the toughest.

My African journey started in 2004, when my partner Zafar Siddiqi and I decided to establish a business-news channel in franchise collaboration with CNBC. What appeared to be a straightforward business case turned out to be a mammoth task, putting together the building blocks in a continent that was immature from a media perspective, both in advertising and distribution, as well as geographically fragmented into 54 diverse countries. Global markets were in chaos from 2008 to 2010, which left the business fraternity in ruins. For start-ups, it was a nightmare. If ever there was a time when I have lost sleep, it was during this period, as the roller coaster of inconsistencies in government actions compounded our woes.

During this tumultuous economic cycle, when the media industry was being battered, I decided to do the unthinkable. I pushed home another franchise opportunity that had been on the back burner for a few years. While print media was collapsing around the world, we launched yet another franchise – *Forbes Africa*.

The opportunity followed my undying belief that the spirit of entrepreneurship in Africa needed to be harnessed and celebrated. After boardroom battles and navigating legal agreements, the magazine was born in October 2011.

A vision will only be a dream until it is successfully implemented. A lot of resources go into implementation, but the most critical one is having the right people who share your vision and are prepared to take a leap of faith and toil to bring the dream to reality. Finding these rare jewels is a journey of a lifetime. I was fortunate enough to find them in our own midst: Chris Bishop as managing editor, and my son, Sid Wahi, as executive director. A soul of a magazine is enshrined in the ethical values of its managing editor and its success in the able hands of an astute business leader who can conceptualise the future. With these two at the helm and a band of loyal soldiers working relentlessly, I was not surprised when *Forbes Africa* rose to become the number-one magazine in its genre on the African continent.

So what does it take to go through stormy waters and bring a ship home safe after a successful mission?

To my mind, there are a lot of factors that play a role. Other than having good people, these include the need for patience, the ability to stay calm through the worst crises and, above all, building interdependence with others. Business has inherent risks, and while we attempt to mitigate these through proactive deeds, you cannot foresee everything. Murphy's Law plays its part again and again and, when you think it's over, it plays it again. The greatest risks of all are those created by man. These can neither be mitigated nor avoided; they need to be managed. To manage risk efficiently, you need to learn how to navigate through apparent irrational conduct through a mastery over the science of human behaviour and emotional intelligence.

We tend to idolise people as role models when we see what they have achieved; often, this is measured by material success. What is never apparent, however, is the journey of blood, sweat and tears. Over the last five years, *Forbes Africa* has covered the inspirational journeys of several business leaders, but, in the process, has also uncovered their trials and tribulations. Those moments of compassion from unexpected quarters, the presence of a son's shoulder, the unscientific hand of Lady Luck, the loyalty from your brothers in arms, and the unwavering belief and faith from your partner, are all summarised in these personal journeys of hope.

And as we get to the pinnacle of our journey and reflect, we must be able to look back not only on the positive influence we've had on the lives of those with whom we have worked, but also on what we were able to give back to those less fortunate than ourselves. Giving back is an integral path of humanity; big or small, this empathetic cord must inherently become our conscience.

Chris Bishop has undertaken to compile the journeys of a number of entrepreneurs through their vicissitudes and how they coped with challenges and adversity to achieve success. To my mind, this compilation is a valuable benchmark and a must-read for all would-be entrepreneurs who want to give up living in a comfort zone and pursue dreaming and building a better future for themselves, their families and for those they have the good fortune to lead.

RAKESH WAHI
FOUNDER & PUBLISHER OF *FORBES AFRICA*
CHAIRMAN OF CMA INVESTMENT HOLDINGS

Acknowledgements

I would like to thank:

The staff at African Business News.
Rakesh Wahi, vice-chairman, African Business News.
The journalists of *Forbes Africa*.
Researchers Jay Caboz, Ancillar Mangena, Jill de Villiers
  and Peace Hyde.

Introduction

'THANK YOU, YOU have changed my life.'
    Scores of people have pushed their way through the rattling crowds in airports, or the din of shopping centres, to shake my hand and utter those words.

I have written for a string of publications and TV stations in the last 36 years, but only *Forbes Africa* has drawn those heartfelt words. These are stories from the horse's mouth, culled from hours and hours of face-to-face interviews and personal encounters; an up-close glimpse into what makes billionaires tick. There is their fierce competitiveness and application on the one side, and, every now and again, their impossible egos on the other.

In this book, we give you the stories of endurance and innovation that have secured these people a fortune; they are full of lessons in business and life. Listen up: it could change your life, too.

These are rich stories, in more ways than one – they are packed with life, laughter and a love of achievement; stories that have proved a catalyst for many lives across Africa.

People often ask me what it is that makes a billionaire. What do I think, from my privileged, close-up view of the movers and shakers in Africa? Some believe that it is all about political connections and rich parents; true, a number of our billionaires do have both, but that is not necessarily the only gateway to success.

What I can say is that success as an entrepreneur requires no specific creed, or colour, or connections, or genetics. It is more about an almost lethal ability to spot an opportunity and to exploit it with ruthless verve and passion.

It is also an ability to lift yourself up from being a tear-sodden heap on the ground and having the inner strength to dust yourself down, jump back up and deliver a vicious left hook; it is to avoid distractions

1

in order to achieve a sort of tunnel vision so that you can see the way forward for your business endeavour.

In entrepreneurship, mental toughness is of more use than a kind bank manager. In fact, many entrepreneurs complain that the banks didn't want to know them when they were struggling; once they had made their millions, of course, the banks were like bees to a honeypot.

Success as an entrepreneur does not often originate from privilege or inherited wealth; poverty is more often the spur.

For a start, most of the entrepreneurs covered in *Forbes Africa* made money because they didn't have any; more than a few grew up barefoot or on the streets before they qualified for a platinum credit card. Tanzanian Reginald Mengi was so poor that he had to sleep with the cattle in his family's tiny hut because they had nowhere else to put them; 40 years later, he has a $550-million fortune.

South African Tim Tebeila had to sell apples on the street to survive; within a decade, he was making millions selling the mining rights beneath his erstwhile bare feet.

Political connections? Sure, most of Africa's entrepreneurs, even those who do not care for politics, have the necessary connections in power. They are as easy to acquire as business cards at a sales convention, and as unavoidable. In many countries, especially the small economies of Africa, the politicians will find you when you have wealth and power, much like the bank managers I mentioned before.

Education? It doesn't matter that much. Many entrepreneurs are erudite and have degrees, but many do not. In fact, quite a few became entrepreneurs after dropping out of school or college. Necessity is often the mother of invention when it comes to entrepreneurs.

When many would-be entrepreneurs were sitting in class pondering the meaning of life, others were out there hustling for their first million. There is an old saying among entrepreneurs that the first lesson in business is to work out how many beans make five; the answer, of course, is five, which illustrates just how simple business really is. When you can work that out, you are 'good to go' – as an increasing number of young entrepreneurs say these days.

Technology? Not all that important. You just need to know how to make money. Mexican Carlos Slim, the second richest man in the world, who made nearly $50 billion through telecoms, hasn't touched a computer in his life and has no intention of ever doing so. He pays others to do that for him, and it doesn't appear to hamper his business acumen. Billionaire Warren Buffett does the same.

Whenever I am asked to speak at functions, I get the same question: Are the super-wealthy born that way, or do they invent themselves?

This question is hard to answer. Mostly, I think it comes down to a personality shaped by both nurture and nature, plus a good dose of experience and a burning desire to get on. This is often driven by a fear of failure, or a strong desire to prove people wrong, or both.

What is also common in many of our stories is how a chance meeting, or a human connection, sparked the money-making fire. Often the entrepreneurial seed can be planted with a stroke of sheer luck. One example is Robert Clyde Packer, one of the richest newspaper magnates Australia has ever seen, whose son, Frank, and grandson, Kerry, both became massive media entrepreneurs in their own right.

According to legend, Robert Packer, the son of a customs official, was a struggling young journalist in his home town of Hobart, Tasmania, in the early 1900s. The story goes that he found a 10-shilling note on the Hobart racecourse and bet it on a horse to win at 13-1. The horse galloped home and won Packer his fare across the Tasman Sea to Australia, where he became a newspaper magnate within two decades.

Failure and disappointment can also propel an entrepreneur from being a mediocre player into a sure-fire success. It is not how often you get knocked down that matters; it is what you do when you get up that does.

Speed of thought and imagination are mandatory, but without hard work and tenacity, all will come to naught.

In short, there seems to be no rhyme or reason to what makes a billionaire, aside from the drive to make money and a personality that can thrive in the worst of times.

There are those who could find a gold mine in their backyard and yet end up penniless. Then there are those who could make money even if the entire planet was flooded by the oceans. They would set up floating desalination plants to sell fresh water to the thirsty masses.

How entrepreneurs grapple with both success and failure is the stuff of *Forbes Africa*. It is the golden thread that binds the magazine and the people we write about to our thousands of readers. *Forbes Africa* is, after all, the creation of an entrepreneur who himself has had tough times and overcome economic adversity.

Operating in the difficult magazine market of Africa, we know the meaning of the word 'struggle'. It is a powerful and privileged position for us to be part of a conversation that could possibly be the salvation of the economies of Africa. Gone are the days when government coffers could create jobs for the people and so solve the unemployment problem; in the 21st century, it is the entrepreneurs who put up their money to pave the way towards greater employment.

This is the conversation that *Forbes Africa* is leading, not only at the top tables, but also in the dusty streets, mines, factories and hair salons of Africa. I have reported from two dozen countries across Africa for more than 20 years, and every time I write a piece, I can visualise the people and where they live and work. Real people with jobs, worries, families and issues who have the courage to dream of a better life.

An NGO called RISE-Ghana, in Bolgatanga in northern Ghana, a few kilometres from the border with the West African nation of Burkina Faso, ships in copies of *Forbes Africa* every month from thousands of kilometres away. When the staff of RISE-Ghana have read them, they donate them to the library, where an estimated 100 schoolchildren thumb through each copy.

What the schoolchildren of Bolgatanga get for their trouble is a no-holds-barred view of business. For we are the drama critics of African business; in fact, many of our roaring stories of capital and chaos, with all the quips along the way, are quite Shakespearean in nature. They are every storyteller's dream, covering the full gamut of the human condition.

Our colleagues at *Forbes* in New York, who have been doing this for nearly a century, have a slightly different take. They say *Forbes* is the shareholder at the back of the annual general meeting who puts up his hand and says: 'Oh, yeah?' We may not have this kind of New York chutzpah, but we have our own African brand of questioning. Our reporters give as good as they get, from Lusaka to Lagos. Their youth, fire and courage are the bedrock of *Forbes Africa*. The reason we get the interviews and stories that make waves is because our journalists travel far, work hard and never give up.

It is how our magazine bucked the trend to become one of the best-read business magazines on the continent – all this in the so-called twilight years of print and in a very tough market. Every month, *Forbes Africa* delves ever deeper into the soul of African business.

At our launch in October 2011, many doomsayers predicted that the magazine stood about as much chance of surviving as a snowball in hell; print journalism was on the wane and advertising was drying up, they said. No one would be even remotely interested in a newcomer on the news stands – surely?

But they were wrong, though it wasn't an easy birth. It took year after year of burning the midnight oil and tons of frustration, many headaches, lots of disappointment and heaps of hard work, as well as nerve-shredding application, to succeed; we endured the slings and arrows of outrageous fortune and stood up defiant.

Our young, vibrant, African-born-and-bred reporters got out there and found enthralling stories to tell, from Maputo and Lusaka to Accra and Lagos and even further afield.

Officials and policemen sometimes tried to stop them, secretaries spurned their calls, competitors tried to force their way past them, petty bureaucrats wanted to dictate terms, and every so often an entrepreneur tried to strong-arm them. No one succeeded in getting in their way. Our journalists have walked through minefields, run the gauntlet of armed poachers, covered thousands of protesters marching against capitalism and encountered tear gas at the gates of government ...

No matter how trying the circumstances, they would record, tran-scribe and verify every word, question and analyse every fact. They smashed stereotypes and rejected the knee-jerk responses of lazy journalism in order to write the real human stories happening in Africa.

Then there were the days they spent in a completely different world, with the rich and famous. It is a rarefied world of fast cars, private jets and wealth beyond anyone's imagination. In Lagos, London and New York, we calculated this wealth, tried to find the secret to creating it, and discovered how easy it is to lose it.

The fruits of our journalists' labour were sweet. Imagine gaining an insight into the thoughts and secrets of billionaires and multimillionaires, listening to their philosophies, recognising their fears and foibles, sympathising with their failures and discussing their future – a masterclass on how to make it.

Not every story always painted a pretty picture – we pride ourselves on digging out both sides of any story. We are nobody's cheerleader. All is fair in business, love and war. If someone deserves criticism, we will provide it; if we don't like something, we will say so and protect our integrity – fiercely. If there is an ardent critic who has clashed with a powerful entrepreneur, we will talk to them.

This gives our growing band of loyal readers what our New York brethren call a 'takeaway'; that is, information that can be used to change your life for the better. Our readers bear this out.

'I have always had the blood of entrepreneurship,' wrote Mike Chilewe, an entrepreneur in Malawi, 'and *Forbes Africa* has helped me so much. *Forbes* helped me get so much interest in acquisitions through the stories of the likes of Tony Elumelu and Mohammed Dewji. I got into it and am now acquiring a company that holds 60 per cent of the food-processing market in Malawi. We are almost done with it now and I owe it to *Forbes Africa*.'

Olushola Pacheco, an entrepreneur in Nigeria, who picked up our magazine while working in London, wrote: '*Forbes Africa* is like the UK Marmite brand with the slogan: love it or hate it. It could remind you about how miserable your life is or just how much work you need to keep putting in to make a success; either way, you can't sit on the fence.'

The hurly-burly of feeding the hungry news beast and producing a quality publication often robs you of the joy and benefit of reflection. That introspection often comes unexpectedly, in the quiet of hearth and home.

'You know what you have done,' said my wife, Tsidi, a veteran business journalist, as we discussed the magazine late one evening. 'You have made our people in Africa household names.'

For so long, the names Branson, Trump, Rockefeller and Slim, synonymous with the word 'entrepreneur', had dominated the headlines in Africa. They were the people that Africans admired and aspired to be (even though at least one of the above couldn't point out Africa on a world map).

But since we started publishing *Forbes Africa*, Dangote, Dewji, Masiyiwa, Ruparelia and Raval have become household names far beyond the countries of their birth.

With this professional footprint in mind, I look back and smile at my first editor's column, way back in 2011, under the headline 'Carpe Diem' – seize the day. It was also my school motto, and I was one of the few who found out what it meant and took it to heart.

I reflected on those barren schooldays as I stiffened the sinews and summoned up the blood to tackle the 600 precious words that would hopefully set the tone for the magazine. It was an honour to write the editor's column; for me, it was a historic, fulfilling moment in my life.

I wrote: 'We will bring you stories of struggle and sacrifice, where fortunes are made and lost, with a sprinkle of precious inside information. We will bring you stories that inspire and warn in equal measure. We want to take readers by the hand and guide them through the boardrooms, markets and clattering factories of this continent.'

On the night we launched, a warm and glittering evening in Johannesburg, South African billionaire Patrice Motsepe unveiled the first ever cover, with his face on it, to cheers and applause. You will read much more about his exploits in this book.

On that night, I said business was the new rock 'n' roll of Africa; I think our readership numbers have proved me right.

As I write this line, I spot a tweet from Reginald Mengi, replying to a young hopeful: 'I've read your tweets u have what it takes to become a successful entrepreneur. Make 2017 a year of action. Exploit opportunities surrounding you.'

So those who have made it in Africa are talking to those who aspire to make it, just another reason why I think the time is ripe for would-be entrepreneurs in Africa to learn and grow.

The personalities who are featured in this book were chosen for a few reasons: one, their extreme wealth: they are either dollar billionaires or multimillionaires (and they are almost all billionaires in rand terms); two, the immense influence they wield in Africa; three, the richness of their stories; and, four, the tenacity they showed in their journey to riches.

I will leave you with a quote from the old man – the late, great Nelson Mandela – that should be inscribed on the wall behind the desk of every powerful person in Africa. I often wonder if he would not have made a great entrepreneur had he not been caught up in law and politics. I think he would have been canny and stubborn when it came to business deals. As much as he was against big-business exploitation in the land of his birth, he always appeared to have a healthy respect for those who spent their lives poring over the books.

In his words: 'Money won't create success; the freedom to make it, will.'

Hear, hear. Let's hope the people featured in *Forbes Africa* – the best-read business magazine on the continent – prove the old man right.

The African roots of *Forbes*

Bertie Charles Forbes

Bertie Charles Forbes

F EW PEOPLE KNOW that the world-famous *Forbes* magazine has roots in Africa, and it always raises eyebrows whenever I relate the background story. This is because hardly anyone knows that the magazine's founder, Scotsman Bertie Charles Forbes, known as BC, years ago gazed up at the stars in the African sky. Like many of the entrepreneurs featured in this book, BC also dared to dream. I managed to piece together Bertie's story by researching the public domain and chatting to his grandchildren, Steve and Kip Forbes, at an editors' conference in New York in 2015.

BC Forbes was one of the many enterprising Scots who spread themselves around the globe in the last few centuries. An entrepreneur, he was driven by a desire to pull himself up by his bootstraps with parsimonious progress. Forbes was a canny Presbyterian, quick with his wits but careful with his money.

'I just write about money, I don't lend it,' was one of his quips when a newsroom colleague asked him for a few dollars at the end of a late-night shift in New York.

'He used to bring us candy when we were kids, but we all knew he used to get it free from the 21 restaurant!' Steve Forbes told me with a chuckle in a hotel on the banks of the Hudson River in New York, 113 years after his grandfather had landed in the United States. Steve Forbes, who ran for US president twice, in 1996 and 2000, and has written a column in his family's magazine for over 40 years, is editor-in-chief of Forbes Media.

One of my former colleagues in Johannesburg, another Scottish journalist, shared with me her theory on why the Scots started wandering the world. 'If you grow up in bad weather and eating boiled turnips, you are desperate to go anywhere!'

It is clear that Forbes saw plenty of turnips and rain in the village of New Deer, Aberdeenshire, a short drive from Aberdeen and the North Sea in the windswept Highlands of north-east Scotland.

At the time of his birth, the population was just under 5 000 and the work was on the land. It is one of many gritty, granite Scottish villages, and it must have been bitingly cold in the winters, which rolled in on the icy wind off the North Sea. About a quarter of a century ago, I reported from that neck of the woods, covering a story of a strike on the North Sea oil rigs off Aberdeen. It was as cold as charity, even though it was summer – you could see your breath in the mornings.

In this cold corner of a cold country, New Deer personifies what many imagine the Highlands to be: rolling, mossy hills and sweet-smelling heather. It was here that Forbes was born, the sixth of 10 children, on 14 May 1880, to Robert Forbes, the village tailor, and Agnes Moir, the blacksmith's daughter.

Forbes, a small child who looked younger than his years, saved the pennies he made from card games and odd jobs. On occasion, he made a few shillings cleaning the mud from the boots of English hunters who came up to Scotland for the shooting season. BC would get up at five in the morning to walk in pitch-darkness to shine 20 pairs of shoes.

At Whitehill Public School in New Deer, Forbes excelled at writing stylish compositions. His English teacher, who used to write a column for a local newspaper, felt he had the makings of a journalist. So Forbes left school at 14 for the nearby fishing village of Peterhead to try to make his name in the world of words and journalism.

In 1894, he signed up for a job as a compositor with the *Peterhead Sentinel* in the belief that it had something to do with writing, only to discover, to his dismay, that it was a printing job to do with ink and metal type. He lamented, then learnt, shorthand. In those days, shorthand was the reporter's only way of recording the spoken word quickly and accurately; it was the mainstay of the trade.

When I started out as a reporter 35 years ago, shorthand speed of at least 100 words per minute and a certificate to verify your achievement were essential for all journalists who hoped for a job on a newspaper.

It meant long evenings of study with a bunch of secretaries at night school. I was so desperate to achieve 100 words per minute that I drilled for many months; I took the examination twice and passed it twice! Even 25 years ago, a newspaper worth its salt wouldn't look at you if you couldn't take down shorthand. It was the only way to cover the court cases and council meetings that were the staple diet of most newspapers. These days, all you need is a phone and the ability to push the record button.

Shorthand helped the young hopeful from New Deer to secure a job as a junior reporter on a larger newspaper, the *Dundee Courier*, in its Perth bureau. In the evenings, BC retired to an iron bed among packing cases in a spartan room. Within a decade, he would wake up in luxury in New York in one of the finest hotels in the world.

A scoop changed BC's life. A careering cattle train crashed through Brechin Station, causing mayhem, killing the animals on board and injuring a number of the crew. Forbes ran to the scene, calmly gathered the necessary information and telephoned his newspaper to alert the editors to make space for the story. He also telephoned flashes to London newspapers, which were to earn him a job as their correspondent in Scotland.

Just as the young reporter's career was taking off, an affair of the heart shot him down. Legend has it that a young woman from a neighbouring village had spurned him, leaving him in 'black, black woe'. Forbes packed his bags and took a ship to the furthest-flung place he could think of – South Africa.

It may have been a decision made in despair, but it wasn't a bad one. At the turn of the 20th century, South Africa, where gold had been uncovered just over a decade before, was a country in flux and expansion. The Witwatersrand Basin – the bed of a prehistoric sea – had dried up millions of years before, leaving rock rich with gold. The so-called buccaneering Randlords like Barney Barnato and Cecil John Rhodes employed armies of low-paid workers to grub out the gold from shafts burrowing deep beneath Johannesburg. Within a decade, gold had transformed the makeshift city from a flimsy tent town into a thriving metropolis with street lights, trams, mansions, music halls and French champagne.

South Africa was also rebuilding in the wake of the Anglo-Boer War, a conflict that assured British supremacy over the colony. There was money to be made by the quick and resourceful who spoke English, the language of business. Forbes believed he could not only nurse his broken heart, but also find excitement and opportunity.

It wasn't as easy as he thought, though; no one had heard of him in South Africa, and few were prepared to give him a chance. He wrote scores of applications to newspapers until, at last, he secured a job on the *Natal Mercury* in Durban. The city, situated on the coast of KwaZulu-Natal, is still one of the biggest and busiest ports in Africa.

In Durban, Forbes settled in quickly as a back-up for the editorial writer. Here he practised and polished his trademark emotive prose. His copy caught the eye of one of the great journalists of his age, who was to give him a leg-up.

Edgar Wallace, born Richard Horatio Edgar Freeman, was a legend in his own time who had borrowed the surname of the man who wrote *Ben-Hur*. Like Forbes, he came from the wrong side of the tracks, worked his way up, and went to South Africa for adventure. He was an extrovert in his youth and grew up to be a flamboyant writer who penned more than 180 novels – an astonishing 18 in one year – while chain-smoking and drinking sugary tea.

Wallace once wrote an 80 000-word novel over a weekend. In his prolific career, he wrote the screenplay for *King Kong* in a purple patch that took him from Johannesburg to Hollywood, where he died, aged 56, from diabetes and pneumonia.

One apocryphal story about Wallace related how a friend had telephoned him, only to be told that he was busy writing his next novel. 'That's okay, I'll wait,' replied the caller.

Wallace had come to South Africa with the British Army and had subsequently bought himself out. He used bush cunning to break the story of the peace treaty that put an end to the Anglo-Boer War, a conflict he covered on horseback. The scoop made his name.

The peace talks were being held amid great secrecy in Vereeniging, just outside Johannesburg. Lord Kitchener, the head of the British Army, tried to keep journalists away, especially Wallace, whom he did not trust. Undeterred, Wallace contacted one of his old army pals, who was a guard inside the peace talks.

Every morning Wallace took the train past the venue and, at the appointed time, the guard would emerge from the tent where the negotiations were taking place and blow his nose with a coloured handkerchief. A red handkerchief meant 'no deal'; yellow meant that the two sides were still talking; and green meant 'peace'. On one of these early-morning train rides, Wallace spotted a green handkerchief and wrote a world exclusive.

Flushed with success, he joined the newly formed *Rand Daily Mail* in Johannesburg – the liberal paper that was to take a firm anti-apartheid stance decades later – where he became editor and columnist. He hired the young Forbes, then in his early 20s, from the *Natal Mercury*.

One quiet Johannesburg evening, another gilt-edged opportunity beckoned. Wallace, who wrote a signed column every night, was away, so Forbes stood in. On that night, he wrote a story about the suicide of a fellow Scot, Hector Archibald MacDonald, a famous British soldier of the late 19th century. MacDonald was born in Dingwall, Rosshire, the son of a poor crofter, and lied about his age to join the Gordon Highlanders. There, he rose rapidly through the ranks, enjoying a glittering military career in India, South Africa and the Sudan. But his personal life was not so salubrious. The official history of the Gordon Highlanders takes up the tale:

> In February 1903 a complaint was made to the Governor, by a clergy-man and some schoolmasters, that Macdonald was in the practice of indulging in inappropriate behaviour with English boys aged 12 or 13. There was also talk of misbehaviour with native boys in a rail-way carriage and another story of indecent exposure. The Governor sent him on leave to England in early 1903 but he was hoping not to see him again. However, Macdonald was ordered to return to

Ceylon to face a court martial. He booked his return passage from Marseilles to Ceylon and checked in to the Regina Hotel in Paris. It was there, on the 25th March, in room 105, that he put a pistol to his head and shot himself.

Forbes wrote a touching eulogy for the *Rand Daily Mail* in his trademark flowery prose: 'Only those who know of the Highlands of Scotland and the clansmen who inhabit its mountains, moors and glens can realize the loss which the Empire will suffer by the downfall of Hector Macdonald.'

The piece concluded: 'I have tried to tell something of his rise, let others write about his fall.'

Everyone at the newspaper commended Forbes on the eulogy, and the editor told him that the Johannesburg Stock Exchange (JSE) had virtually stopped for an hour while traders discussed it.

But Johannesburg, for all its gold and riches, was too small and provincial for Forbes, and he set sail for New York late in 1903. He spent most of his savings and the money his colleagues had collected for him as a farewell gift on sailing first class, even though he couldn't really afford it, because he felt you had to mix with the right people – rich and powerful people – to get on ... a theme that ran throughout his life.

In 1904, when Forbes arrived at Ellis Island, in the shadow of the Statue of Liberty, he came under the scrutiny of the immigration inspectors along with the huddled masses from around the world, all of them yearning for freedom. Between 1892 and 1954, 12 million people passed through Ellis Island. They paused for several hours for inspection in the so-called 'hall of tears', where immigrants were informed whether they would be allowed to start a new life in the United States or be sent back to wherever they were trying to escape from. The joke went that if you could walk, you were in; 98 per cent of those who set foot on Ellis Island were allowed into the US. Forbes was one of them.

'He had 50 bucks in his pocket, so the guys told him he was unlikely to be a burden on the state and let him in!' his grandson, Kip Forbes, chuckled. We were sitting in a hotel in New Jersey, overlooking Ellis Island, more than a century later. Kip's mother had named him Christopher but didn't want people to call him Chris, so she nick-named him Kip.

Like most of the Forbes brothers, Kip is urbane, wedded to the family business and expensively educated. He went to private school, then Princeton University. Like the rest of his family, Kip loves collect-ing objets d'art, with a particular interest in Napoleon III. He has spent a fortune acquiring portraits and objets relating to the leader of France's second empire, including Napoleon III's hat, which he sold in 2014 for €1.9 million.

More than 100 years ago, Kip's grandfather, BC Forbes, fresh off the boat on Ellis Island, could only dream of such vast wealth, but he had every intention of making it.

In his first weeks in New York, finding a job, never mind a new life, proved a struggle for Forbes. No one cared about his writing or work experience; almost no one had heard of the *Rand Daily Mail*. On top of that, Forbes didn't even look like the urbane, up-and-coming New York journalist that he so desperately wanted to be. A friend advised him to dress in pinstripe trousers and a black morning coat, which made him look older. It was a uniform that was to become his for life. Then fate also lent a hand, on the golf course of all places.

One day, Forbes went to play golf. As he waited for his partner to arrive, a wealthy golfer mistook him for a caddy. Forbes, always with an eye for an opportunity, played along and carried the man's clubs around the entire course. The rich golfer and the penniless journalist started talking, and by the 18th hole they had hatched a plan to intro-duce Forbes to fellow Scot John Doddsworth, the managing editor of *Journal of Commerce and Commercial Bulletin*. Forbes met with him and offered to work for free.

'He didn't know whether the guy would take his free labour and toss him out, but it worked,' says Steve Forbes. 'He got the job and he was so full of energy, my grandfather, that he went to another newspaper under a different name and got a job there too. Probably one of his happiest moments in life was when the two editors got into an argument over who had the best business reporter – it was my grandfather in both cases.'

Forbes ended up writing about dry goods, which, he lamented, lived up to their name. It may have been a lean spell for creative writing, but Forbes seized the opportunity to inveigle himself among the rich and influential.

Even though he couldn't afford it, he moved into the Waldorf Astoria on Manhattan's Fifth Avenue, the playground of the rich and famous.

'He probably had the smallest room at the back of the hotel,' Steve Forbes said, 'but every night he would be there in the bar, with his morning coat on, mixing with all the important people.'

Kip recalled his grandfather's tart sense of humour, especially concerning money. He told me about a woman who used to live next door to his childhood home. She was spending a small fortune to have a swimming pool built in her backyard. Those were the days when swimming pools were an expensive rarity.

'[My grandfather] took one look through the back window and said: "If she is spending that kind of money, clearly she hasn't got it,"' Kip said with a smile.

BC Forbes was the life and soul of many parties and poker games in New York, according to his grandchildren. Along the way he garnered a good deal of respect for his ability as a journalist. He was the man New York's most powerful industrialists and entrepreneurs wanted to talk to. In the process, he found that most entrepreneurs were a lot more interesting than the businesses they had founded. This fascination with the inner thoughts of rich and powerful entrepreneurs is the hallmark of *Forbes* magazine more than a century later.

Eventually, Forbes wanted to launch his own magazine, which he was going to call *Doers and Doings* (one wonders whether this title would have stood the test of time). In the end, the founder was persuaded to use his own respected name, and he took the plunge on 15 September 1917.

'He raised the money and decided to launch,' according to Steve Forbes. 'The timing was probably not the most fortuitous, as it was in the midst of World War I, but the [magazine] worked from the very beginning.'

A century on, *Forbes* sells more than six million copies every issue and is the best-read business magazine in the United States.

Forbes Africa is the best-read business magazine on this continent. Both have advanced the discussion of business; both were, in some way, born from dreaming under the African stars.

2

The richest man in Africa

Aliko Dangote

Aliko Dangote

W HEN IT COMES to entrepreneurs, there is always one lion that rules the jungle, the one who is both feared and respected; the one everyone wants to meet and against whom would-be entrepreneurs measure themselves.

In Africa, that man is Aliko Dangote – the biggest name in business on the continent, the billionaire who believes that to live is to be an entrepreneur and encourages others to follow in his footsteps. More than that, he is a *guerrilla* entrepreneur – the Che Guevara of African business, but in a sober suit. Dangote believes passionately in Afri-capitalism, and he promotes it passionately. In his opinion, Africans can raise themselves out of poverty through hard work, sound business acumen and by taking calculated risks. In this, he believes, Nigerians are the front line leading the way into battle. He yearns for the day when foreign investors will no longer be seen as the be-all and end-all for Africa.

Fleet Street has called Dangote the second most powerful black man in the world after Barack Obama. *Forbes* estimated his personal fortune at $12.2 billion in 2017, making him twice as wealthy as Chelsea FC owner Roman Abramovich, and probably twice as ambitious. For Dangote is planning a bid to buy his favourite premier-league football club, Arsenal, and, if he gets what he wants, the fans could be in for an interesting ride. At the very least, the grass will not grow under Arsenal's feet if Dangote, who rarely does things by half, buys his way into the boardroom in North London.

Dangote was taken to watch Arsenal more than 30 years ago by its then chairman, David Dein, a former sugar trader. According to London's *Daily Mail*, Dein had helped Dangote get his sugar business off the ground in 1980. Three decades later, Dangote Sugar Refinery Plc accounts for more than 90 per cent of the Nigerian market.

Acquiring Arsenal is just another dream, on another day, for an entrepreneur who sleeps just three hours a night, rising at 5 a.m. to brainstorm his next move. His tax affairs are tidy, and compliance to regulations and corporate governance robust in a business that has afforded him scores of homes, private jets, polo ponies and luxury cars. When Dangote is chauffeur-driven to work at his company's headquarters in Lagos, the children wave from the streets as if he were royalty.

On first meeting Dangote, as I did on a muggy afternoon in Lagos in 2012, he struck me as a highly understated billionaire. He is soft-spoken, very formal, and keeps his hands clasped in front of him like a school principal rather than a tycoon. His suit is neat and conservative – almost as conservative as *Forbes*'s estimate of his wealth, which he believes is way short of the mark.

'*Forbes* works on listed assets and we have a lot of companies that are not listed, but they are on their way to being listed,' he told me at his headquarters in Union Marble House, in the plush suburb of Ikoyi, opposite the main Falomo roundabout in the heart of Lagos, hinting that he owns more assets than *Forbes* will ever know.

Whatever its value, the fruits of Dangote's fortune are spectacular as well as sweet. Their roots can be traced to the three words inscribed on a plaque that holds pride of place on a table in his office: 'Nothing Is Impossible'.

'That is my mantra in life,' he says. 'No matter what you go through, just remember that nothing is impossible for you to achieve and you will overcome it.'

This confidence belies a humble beginning in business nearly half a century ago in the northern Nigerian city of Kano, where he grew up surrounded by wealth and royalty and turned his first penny. Dangote was born into a Hausa Muslim family, and his first entrepreneurial act was to sell sweets on the streets of the town. He chuckles when he tells me that, actually, as he was from a well-to-do family, *he* bought the sweets and got his servants to sell them!

In 1977, Dangote's life changed forever when his enterprising uncle, Sani Dangote, took him under his wing and employed him in the commodities trade, which was opening up as Nigeria found its post-independence feet.

Dangote was 20 when he approached his uncle with a business plan. Sani lent his nephew 500 000 naira to get him started, but also offered him a lifetime of free advice. The deal was that Dangote would pay back the money in three months.

He started small and began trading, importing necessities such as sugar, rice, pasta, salt, cotton, millet, cocoa, textiles and vegetable oil. He moved south to Lagos and began traversing the country to set up a distribution network. This not only ensured that his company delivered goods faster than his competitors, but it also sharpened the young man's now legendary networking and negotiating skills, which would prove vital in breaking into the big time.

To cut a long story short, Dangote paid back his loan within the stipulated three months and then sank his energy into building one of Africa's biggest and most successful companies, the Dangote Group.

The next step in creating his business empire was cement. This was the commodity that would produce the building blocks for Dangote's bridge to the big time. Africa grows by the day, and it needs tons of cement to build its houses, offices and factories. Dangote anticipated the demand, used his networking skills to secure a licence and began to import cement.

Importing cement through terminals in Lagos and Port Harcourt was basically a licence to print money in those heady days, as the rapidly expanding country couldn't get enough of it. But Dangote wanted even more. He soon realised that the whole of Africa was crying out for cement; there was a fortune to be made in exporting it.

Those close to Dangote say that the watershed moment in his career was his decision to manufacture and export cement rather than merely importing it – but it was also almost the end of him.

In 2002, Dangote made a bold move. He decided to build his own cement factory, in northern Nigeria. It was a shrewd decision, taking advantage of government subsidies allotted to companies that would make Nigeria self-sufficient in cement.

'At the time, the entire production of Nigeria was less than two million tons, but we decided that we were going to go ahead and build a five-million-ton capacity,' he recalls.

Many entrepreneurs in Africa will tell you how minor details can derail a project, and so it was with Dangote and his cement plant: an incorrect soil test almost ruined his plans before he had even started.

'Normally the northern part of Nigeria has very hard ground. But [the experts] came back and said we just needed a shallow foundation of a maximum of two metres. So the drawing and everything was done based on a two-metre foundation. When we were three months into the job, we realised it was more than this,' says Dangote.

This marked the beginning of a long battle to salvage the multi-million-dollar project upon which Dangote had bet the ranch. And it was about to get worse. Dangote had decided not to do a proper feasibility study, so as to avoid unwanted attention from his competition. It proved an expensive risk to take, as no one was quite sure what was needed to build the cement factory.

'So, now we had to go and do piling. We had to stop and change all the drawings and, all of a sudden, we were faced with 1000 piles that had to be built, and there were not enough rigs in Nigeria. So we had to order new rigs and even buy rigs for some of the contractors,' Dangote recalls.

While the workers were sweating over the rigs, Dangote was scratching his head, trying to come up with the nearly half a billion dollars he needed to complete the factory.

'We needed to raise $480 million, but the problem was that 90 per cent of the banks at the time had a market capital of only $20 million. In addition, there were no long-term loans, only short-term loans for about 90 days, so you can see what challenge we faced. The project stopped, we had to change the drawings and we could not borrow too much money in the system. Borrowing short term and investing in a long-term business was so difficult.'

There was another problem – a lack of energy. The Nigerian government had promised to build a gas pipeline to power the area back in 1978, but it never came to fruition.

'So we had to construct a 92-kilometres gas pipeline. The water table was very bad in the area, so we had to build a dam and over 100 houses, because there was nothing there. So the challenges were coming one by one.'

Dangote looks around his office in Lagos more than a decade later and gestures towards the wall. 'I had the project drawings on the wall in my office, but I knew that once this project fails, the group is gone, and that is what really kept me going. It was a major project for us, because our size compared to a project of half a billion was big money for us then.'

As Dangote trudged down a very dark tunnel, he saw a faint, flickering light at the end of it. The International Finance Corporation (IFC), a subsidiary of the World Bank, came up with $479 million for the Dangote cement plant. It may have been of some comfort, but the costs were still ballooning, threatening once again the very survival of the business.

'The most challenging [moment] was when we had the cost overrun. Now we had finished the cement factory and the factory was not working, and that was really when I went from black into red. I knew that we were really in trouble. But we were adamant and we persevered. We had challenges for over a year or so, and the factory was working on and off.'

By 2003 the cement factory was finally completed and, in time, it started to prosper. It now exports cement to 18 countries in sub-Saharan Africa and as far away as Nepal. With its rising revenue, it is the cornerstone of the Dangote Group's success. The company now has operations in Nigeria, Benin, Ghana, Congo, Tanzania, Senegal, South Africa and Zambia.

'It was a challenging experience, and that is why I have the plaque on the table that says nothing is impossible. You need tenacity and focus in business. I have learnt a lot, and since that time I don't really get scared of anything.'

This confidence has contributed to Dangote's reputation as the king of the Nigerian Stock Exchange (NSE), one of Africa's most vibrant and robust bourses. It hums along, whatever the international economic weather, in downtown Lagos amid hooting horns and the rumble of bumper-to-bumper traffic. It was here on a hot, sweaty afternoon in 2012 that I caught up with Dangote to talk about Africa, entrepreneurs, terrorism and investment for a *Forbes Africa* cover story. He is a hard man to pin down, always a hop, skip and jump away from the next private-jet flight to a power meeting. Getting Africa's richest man on the cover was an important milestone for the fledgling *Forbes Africa* magazine. Many of our readers say that they only started buying the magazine once we had bagged the lion. On that day in Lagos, we chased him as hard as if he were the yeti in the Himalayas. But it would be worth all the hustling.

The NSE had invited Dangote to ring its closing bell at the end of the day's trade, which was a great honour. Dangote was positioned on a platform above the trading floor with a crowd of jumping, joyful, noisy traders at his feet. The traders had a right to be pleased with themselves, as it had been another fruitful day on this vibrant emerging-market trading floor, which never seemed affected by recession. On this day alone, 4 483 trades took place and 2.62 billion naira changed hands; everyone said it had been an exceptional session.

The traders wore maroon jackets with big buttons, which appeared almost ecclesiastical. As Dangote stepped up to ring the bell, they burst into cheers and applause.

'My name is Aliko Dangote. You may know my name. We are doing quite a lot here,' he played to the crowd.

'More, more, more!' the traders shouted back, waving their arms high in the air and dancing from foot to foot. Take the jackets away, and it could have been a wedding or a football crowd.

Never mind George Soros – George Clooney would have struggled to draw the acclaim afforded Dangote on that day. For Dangote's companies make up the lion's share of business on the NSE, and everyone who has ever sold a share there goes to sleep at night safe in that knowledge. Dangote made a short speech, swearing loyalty to Africa, his country and the stock exchange for evermore. He was literally shining over his constellation of stocks and shares that had made so many so rich.

The euphoria reached a crescendo as the cement and commodities king lifted the bell and rang it above his head. All around me swirled a sea of open faces, rapt to the last man and woman. Little did they know that at that very instant, Dangote was planning to list thousands of miles away in icy London; in the heat of this Lagos moment, no one seemed to care.

The London event happened weeks later, on 2 April 2012, when his $11-billion cement business was listed on the London Stock Exchange (LSE). It was the first time the company had listed outside of Nigeria, its purpose to raise money for the Dangote Group's ambitious expansion plans across Africa.

In Lagos, I stood back and surveyed one of the richest billionaires on the planet as he smiled and shook hands on the stage. It felt like a holiday all round as everyone basked in the reflected glory of Africa's richest man, who was also one of their own.

The final event of the day occurred in a small room when Dangote and the head of the NSE, Oscar Onyema, and his cohorts, took their places behind a table to answer questions from the Nigerian media. Then some photographs were taken before, at last, Dangote sat down in front of me with a cup of tea.

He struck me as a modest man; you could walk past him in the street without looking at him twice. Everything, from his suit to his demeanour, was understated. For a man who was about to invest $70 billion in Africa in the middle of a recession, he appeared very cool and unruffled.

'The first priority is to export,' he told me. 'If you look at it, we have built some factories across West Africa and some of them are still under construction. The main intention for us is to export to the continent out of Nigeria to the other West African countries, because when you export from Nigeria, you enjoy the export incentive, which is about 30 per cent. You also enjoy the non-payment of duty in the other various destinations ... We are thinking about targeting five million tons in exports.'

Dangote agreed that Nigeria was facing troubled times. In the weeks leading up to our interview, there had been widespread unrest in Lagos when fuel subsidies, which for years had made petrol for motorists dirt cheap, were cancelled. Worse still, bombs had gone off in the north of the country amid talk of secession. Not a pretty picture, I said to Dangote.

'I am not really concerned,' he countered. 'Most of these challenges that we are facing today ... there are several other countries that are facing the same challenges and they are doing very well economically. Turkey had the same issue a few months back. There were bombings, but the government rose to the challenge and they were able to pipe everything down. So I believe that in Nigeria we will do the same,' says Dangote, who believed this sincerely at the time of the interview. Hindsight may be a wonderful thing, but the troubles of Turkey have proven even more challenging than those of Nigeria.

Then there was the lack of electric power. Power stations in Nigeria are decrepit, and the thermal-coal industry – usually the cheap prop to generate power across Africa – was almost non-existent in a land where oil is king. A plan to revive the coal mines had failed miserably. Dangote agreed that the lack of power was holding back his country.

But, he said, 'I think the real issue is that people are actually under-rating the economy of Nigeria. You will see the economy of Nigeria at work when we are able to deliver power. By the time we are able to deliver power, I can assure you that we will be having double GDP growth. Take Kano, the state where I come from, for example. We have a small amount of power that is shared amongst 17 to 18 million people. If you empower them, you will definitely see a massive difference.'

When I mentioned the word 'entrepreneurs' – Nigerian entrepreneurs in particular – I could see a glint in Dangote's eyes for the first time. This is his pride and passion. He sees his countrymen as the special forces of business in Africa with the ability to parachute in anywhere and make money.

'I went to Brazil on business the other week, and I went out to buy something and the first shop I went to was run by a Nigerian,' he chuckled. 'You see, a Nigerian by nature does not work for anybody. A Nigerian will always do his best to work for himself, and if you empower them, you will be shocked by what this economy can do. It will be much more than the boom of telecoms, where in 2000 we had only 436 000 lines, and this year we have more than 96 million. So it is going to happen, it will come …

'There are so many opportunities in Africa, but people out there, outside of Africa, who have real money to invest, will not come and invest unless they see the locals invest in their own economy. If we don't invest, they will always believe that there is something that they cannot see, which we, the locals, are seeing – that is why we are not investing. So it is a priority, it is of top urgency for us to start investing and have confidence in our own system and economies, so that others may follow. We saw it happen in our sector of cement, when we started pumping in a lot of money. Others who were not serious about investing are now in.'

Dangote really does believe that Nigeria, despite all its problems, should be holding masterclasses on how to be entrepreneurs for the rest of the continent.

According to him, 'It is for them [Nigerians] to partner with other African brothers and sisters to make sure they show them the way, how we have negotiated our economy. When you look at our economy 25 years back, it was controlled by Indians and Lebanese. Right now, almost 90 per cent of our economy is in our own hands; we are making it happen. A lot of companies, like the Heinekens, Nestlés, Unilever, etc., they are pumping a lot of money [into Nigeria], because they have seen that we, the locals, are also heavily investing our money in the system.'

Many will be surprised to hear that Dangote wants to give most of his fortune away. Like many billionaires, he has his own foundation that funnels money to those who need it. The Dangote Foundation was founded nearly 23 years ago, long before Dangote hit the jackpot, and he has donated more than a billion dollars to it. The foundation grants cash – sometimes as little as $80 – to would-be entrepreneurs at grassroots level, and complements Nigeria's poverty alleviation efforts.

In 2012, he gave $500 000 to the victims of a deadly blast at a munitions factory in Congo Brazzaville. He made it clear to me that he wants to go much further in transferring his wealth.

'As a businessman and entrepreneur, I want to be remembered for doing a lot of massive, challenging things and succeeding at them, but I think I would like to be remembered more in terms of doing charitable things. As soon as I deliver on most of my projects, I intend to give most of my money back to society,' he told me.

'I don't know what percentage of my fortune I will give away, because, you know, I have three top kids and they must try to fight me before anything can happen.'

Dangote's next business step will be into the uncertain and volatile oil market.

'We have been pushed into oil because we realised that we had too much cash for the type of business we are running today, so we need to diversify. For the diversification strategy, we look at the areas that can actually take Nigerians to the next level, and that is where we map out all the issues and the problems that we are facing, as a country, for lack of diversifying the economy,' he said.

The Dangote Group is building one of the largest oil refineries in the country, which on completion will not only have the capacity to meet Nigeria's requirement of 445 000 to 550 000 barrels of fuel, but have spare capacity to export, according to Dangote. The project is expected to be completed by 2018. One of the issues that negatively impacts Africa's oil industry is its lack of refineries. As a result, oil is often shipped out of the continent to be refined and then shipped back, at great cost.

Ironically, it was fuel that would terminate one of Dangote's dream projects as 2016 drew to a close, when he was forced to shut down his $500-million cement plant in Mtwara, Tanzania, in the south-east of the country. Dangote had built the cement plant based on a promise the government had made to provide cheap natural gas – which would be extracted near Mtwara – to run it. The promise of subsidised fuel evaporated when the government changed hands and President John Magufuli replaced President Jakaya Kikwete in 2016.

The plant was forced to run on diesel generators, which left Dangote with a huge fuel bill that allegedly cost his company $4 million a month. They tried to import South African coal to fill the energy gap, but that just upset the Tanzanian authorities even more. They argued that Tanzania had cheaper coal at home, but Dangote's people complained that the coal, mined in the Songwe region, hundreds of kilometres from the Mtwara plant, was of poor quality.

In August 2016, Tanzania banned coal imports in a move seen as a dig at Dangote. That December, Dangote shut down the Mtwara cement plant, thus putting the ball back in the government's court. One can't miss the message from the man who can be as ruthless in business as he is benevolent: no cheap energy, no Africans investing in Africa. As 2016 drew to a close, a new deal on providing gas to Mtwara was being negotiated.

Was this a wake-up call for Africapitalism? Maybe. But you can be sure that Dangote is a survivor. He started his business empire selling sugar nearly 40 years ago, and he will hit the sweet spot in business yet again. Who knows, he might even buy Arsenal ...

3

The young Tsar of Dar

Mohammed Dewji

Mohammed Dewji

LIFE LOOKS GOOD from the 20th floor of the dockside office of billionaire Mohammed Dewji, the slender, hungry young man who wants to be the richest man in Africa. When the sun shines over Tanzania and the sky is blue, it is the kind of view that tempts you to think that anything is possible. In fact, when Dewji began his journey to billions, he had the misguided notion that he could be the Tiger Woods of Tanzania, but more on that later.

From high up here, the young Tsar of Dar, not far past his 40th birthday, surveys his kingdom. It is a busy day for Dewji. He is on his way to a press conference, the topic of which will be football. The saying goes that buying a soccer club is a quick way to turn a big fortune into a small one. It is one of the many problems on Dewji's plate as he sits behind his desk preparing his notes for the press conference on the new acquisition that will compromise his bank balance overnight. The stunning panorama below him displays the busy docks of Dar es Salaam, set against the backdrop of the sparkling-blue Indian Ocean. The docks and the ocean beyond are reminders both of the poverty from which Dewji's ancestors came and the fortune he hopes to attain.

For a start, it is from these docks that tons of goods, manufactured in Tanzania by an army of workers, are exported every day, earning Dewji's family business millions of dollars every week. From being a relative unknown, this business has resulted in Dewji now being the 16th-richest billionaire, with an estimated worth of $1.4 billion, on the continent.

It is a rich harvest for the young workaholic and influential pan-African entrepreneur who puts in 100 hours a week and attends 60 board meetings a month. Unlike other successful entrepreneurs in Africa, he did not accumulate most of his wealth from dealing in commodities, or from trading – it came from producing necessities for Africa. This cuts down on the millions this continent spends on importing bare essentials, like food and cloth, every year. For that reason, *Forbes Africa* elected Dewji as our Person of the Year in 2015.

In his minimalist high-rise office with its polished surfaces and black leather couches, Dewji plots businesses in a dozen African countries in search of his target of $5 billion in revenue a year – his Holy Grail. As part of his ambitious plans, he aims to give Coca-Cola a bloody nose.

The ocean far below recalls the perilous journey his grandparents had endured when they set off in a dhow from Gujarat in western India to escape grinding poverty. According to family legend, a kind wind blew them across the Indian Ocean to the coast of Zanzibar, where they found little more than they had left behind in India, but at least their lives were spared. The couple journeyed south, mostly on foot, to the town of Singida, in central Tanzania, about 670 kilometres west of Dar es Salaam.

It was in the impoverished Singida that the family set up a small trading business, in a hut made from mud and cement, which they also called home. They made a living by buying a particular commodity, like rice, breaking it down into smaller units and selling it retail. This simple, homespun business strategy, coupled with thrift, would be the origin of the multibillion-dollar family-owned conglomerate MeTL.

Mohammed Dewji's birth in this tiny family home was as humble and difficult as that of the family business.

'I was born at home with a midwife [in attendance], as my mom didn't make it to the hospital in time. She went through 18 hours of labour. They did not realise that the umbilical cord was around my neck, and I wasn't coming out. The hospital was about 60 kilometres away and the roads were terrible. It would have taken my parents a couple of hours to get there. Finally, I made it,' says Dewji, sitting in his high leather chair in a skyscraper a world away from Singida.

In the 1970s, Mohammed's father, Gulam Dewji, laid the foundations of what would become the giant MeTL by setting up an import-export trading business. By diligently applying himself to the business for a quarter of a century, Gulam Dewji amassed an estimated personal fortune worth $560 million.

He raised his son in the business. Mohammed Dewji may have spent his high-school years in the United States, but his business education happened at home.

'Every Christmas and summer, when I would come back to Tanzania, my father would make me come to the office and show me what he did and how he ran his business. He took me to China when I was 11 years old; we travelled to seven cities. I met a lot of businessmen and -women. He incorporated and indoctrinated that thought process of entrepreneurship into me from a very young age,' Dewji remembers.

Being schooled at his father's knee has left its imprint on Dewji. Despite his vast wealth and influence, he comes across like your younger brother's best friend. I met him in Johannesburg in 2012, when MeTL signed for a $100-million bank loan. It took me about 10 minutes to work out who the billionaire in the room was, as Dewji was approaching everyone, shaking hands, showing respect. He seemed almost eager to please. As usual, he was prepared to talk at length – and with great excitement and humility – about his business. It was only when he spoke about MeTL that I realised who he was.

Dewji Snr, despite raising his son with a firm hand, allowed the young man to chase his dreams far from the boardroom, even though those dreams may have seemed frivolous to a hard-headed businessman.

Dewji started playing golf from a young age, a game he loved with a passion, and he dreamt of becoming the Tiger Woods of Tanzania. At primary school, he played off a handicap of three. On the strength of his talent, his father enrolled him in the prestigious Arnold Palmer Golf Academy in Orlando, Florida.

'I won the regional competitions,' Dewji recalls, 'but when we got to the national competitions, I saw younger players hitting the ball further and straighter than me, and I decided I wasn't going to make it.' The fact that he no longer plays the game at all says something about his nature. If he can't win, he'll do something else.

This was the first of two events that would lead Dewji back to the family business and to making his own fortune. As a consolation for giving up golf, Dewji went to study business and theology at Georgetown University, Washington – the alma mater of former US president Bill Clinton, former president of the Philippines, Gloria Arroyo, and former First Lady of the US, Jacqueline Kennedy.

'Georgetown really moulded me,' Dewji says. 'It took me a step forward. I understood that you need to be dreaming, but not daydreaming. You need to try to dream a reality. Then you have vision.'

The hard-working Dewji left quite an impression on one of his tutors at Georgetown.

Recalls Pietra Rivoli, the deputy dean of Georgetown University's McDonough School of Business, who taught Dewji international finance: 'While other students tried to stay awake through discussions of exchange rates, Mohammed would stay after class to talk about how the readings might pertain to the Tanzanian shilling, and how Tanzania could address its economic challenges. Even at the age of 20 or so, he was thinking about how to improve life in his country.'

A brief career as a Wall Street trader followed, until a second event propelled him home. It happened during a telephone call from New York to Tanzania.

'I asked my father for money to buy a suit for work. He said if I couldn't afford a suit, it was time for me to come home and work for him!' chuckles Dewji.

He returned to Tanzania in 1999. Fresh from the US, Dewji entered the boardroom and learnt the ropes studiously. All eyes in the company must have been on this precocious son of the boss with his fancy education. But Mohammed soon proved his mettle and his father handed him the reins, making him one of the youngest CEOs in Africa, at just 29. Dewji is still as full of idealism, and with an unshakable belief in his country and its free-market reforms, as he was at that young age.

'We've been growing at 7 per cent. I mean, this country is so blessed: you talk about gold, we have it. You talk about iron, coal, we have it,' he says in his enthusiastic, machine-gun-paced way whenever he talks business.

At the helm of the family business, Dewji started transforming MeTL into a pan-African conglomerate with operations in Tanzania, Uganda, Malawi, Zambia and Mozambique. He bought up loss-making government-owned textile and edible-oil plants, leftovers from the country's failed socialist past under the late President Julius Nyerere, with the intention of turning them around.

'I bought a lot of sick industries, which included soap production, grain milling, rice and sugar blending. I also went into the edible-oil business and the textile industry,' Dewji explains.

Nearly 18 years on, he owns the biggest edible-oil refinery in Africa, and runs a diversified group that includes the manufacturing and distribution of everything from soap to salt, fertiliser, motorcycles, bubble gum, yeast, ballpoint pens and fruit juice. In all, the MeTL Group manufactures and sells more than 200 commodities in East, Central and southern Africa.

'We mainly deal in FMCGs [fast-moving consumable goods],' Dewji tells me. '[These goods] touch people's lives; they are needed by the common man.'

The group also exports 50 of its own brands, taking advantage of the fact that Tanzania borders eight countries. Distribution has proven to be a huge task. In a vast country like Tanzania, which measures a million square kilometres and where 80 per cent of the population live in far-flung villages, getting the products to the people is a real challenge. However, with more than a hundred trade outlets countrywide, MeTL Group has managed to undercut multinational giants like Unilever and drive them from the East African nation.

'I have a big basket of goods,' Dewji smiles. 'I have warehousing and logistics. I have over a thousand trucks. Everything complements each other. It's very difficult for people to come from the outside and compete with me.

'I had an advantage, because I started off with capital. For others, it's very difficult. That's why people keep on asking me, "Mohammed, are you successful because you grew the business together with your father from a $30-million-revenue business to one of one and a half billion dollars?" I tell them [my father] is far smarter [than me] because he created something out of nothing. I may have quadrupled it and done very well, but he started with no capital.'

Nevertheless, capital – or the lack of it in Dar es Salaam – was a hurdle the young Dewji had to jump early on in his business career. Despite the fact that he had significant capital behind him, he needed a lot more for his investment plans. He realised that the banks in Tanzania were years behind when it came to liberalisation of the economy and far too small to lend the amounts MeTL needed.

'I remember that one multinational bank could lend me a maximum of $8 000. They could not lend more than 20 per cent of their core capital to one customer. This was a big challenge, because I could not grow without having capital and without getting into debt. During those days, private equity investment was weak, so I actually went to South Africa and started pitching,' he says.

His pitches resulted in hundreds of millions in loans from South African banks, allowing him to step up his acquisitions and investments, a drive based on tough number-crunching and an instinct for finding hidden value in companies.

One sector Dewji tried to resuscitate was Tanzania's ailing textile industry. Knowing that the East African nation is the continent's third largest cotton producer, he decided to buy and refurbish four rundown mills, three in Tanzania and one in Mozambique. His next foray will be into Zambia and Malawi, he says, followed by Ethiopia.

'We were quite lucky. Tanzania's previous socialist government had invested hundreds of millions of dollars in infrastructure to build textile mills. But under socialism, everything collapsed. So we were able to acquire these industries very cheaply. Obviously the machinery was rundown, the technology obsolete. We had to rehabilitate the mills by investing in top European and American machinery.'

With the result that the MeTL Group is now sub-Saharan Africa's largest textile player, integrating the entire value-addition chain from ginning to spinning, weaving, processing and printing.

'The total capacity of our three textile mills in Tanzania and

Mozambique is over 100 million metres of cloth, which is about 100 000 kilometres of cloth, the equivalent of two times the circumference of the earth. We also went into bicycle and matchbox manufacturing, and so on and so forth. So, there's a lot of manufacturing that we got into during my time, which has brought in a lot of value and created a lot of jobs.'

Thanks to Dewji's entrepreneurial vigour, Tanzania is able to compete with the world's largest and cheapest textile producer, China – at least within its own borders, where government policies, including import tariffs on textiles and a standard value added tax (VAT) of 18 per cent, help protect home-grown industry.

'Today, overall textile production is cheaper in Tanzania than in China. Labour is competitive in terms of pricing. Tanzania's big advantage is that we have cotton, while China has to import it. So they cannot compete with me in my market,' explains Dewji.

Helmut Engelbrecht, head of investment banking in Africa at Standard Bank, one of the financial institutions working with the MeTL Group, says, 'If I think of a top African businessman, Mohammed comes to mind. He works very long hours, is always on the move, has an eye for opportunity and a very good business sense. He is level-headed and pays extremely close attention to detail.'

A snapshot of Dewji's shrewd modus operandi can be taken from his foray into the sisal business.

'We contribute about 40 per cent of all the sisal in this country. I have integrated into sisal bags, but I want to go into carpeting, sisal yarn and sisal biodegradable. [Sisal] has many brilliant characteristics – people now use it in gypsum board in building, and for strengthening in the vehicle and jet industries. They even use it in skateboards. We have moved away from the orthodox uses of just twines and ropes; now we have multiple uses and, if you go to Europe and Wall Street, you will see these beautiful sisal carpets that cost thousands and thousands of dollars a ton. This is the sisal that I'm talking about.'

All this ambition would have been useless without the timely purchase of a large sisal-processing plant. At the time it was running at break-even, with prices of around $300 a ton for sisal, producing every-thing from ropes to coffee bags. Dewji estimated that his production costs would rise from $300 to around $700, but he also suspected that prices were going to increase. And they did, to $2100. Now MeTL is exporting 8000 tons of sisal a year at a handsome profit.

Dewji has also been pouring money into many other sectors, includ-ing agriculture, an industry from which many investors shy away. MeTL owns 50000 hectares of arable land, making it the largest private land-owner in Tanzania. Aside from sisal, it owns tea gardens and cashew fields, which are good cash generators. Nearly all the cashew kernels are exported, for hard currency, to the United States.

Always thinking a few steps ahead, Dewji has been making plans to profit from the land he owns. Dar es Salaam, a city of 4.4 million people, is growing in leaps and bounds. So Dewji is turning a 17000-acre plot that he bought cheaply several years ago, situated 25 kilometres outside the capital, into a dry-port with an internal container depot. From there, a railway connection will feed into Dar es Salaam's massive harbour, which is slowly but surely running out of space. It will, of course, also generate huge profits.

'My philosophy as a businessman is not to be satisfied with what I've got, but to always work harder to achieve more,' he says.

Dewji's business instincts and application have also led MeTL into the competitive fuel market in Tanzania. In a mere three and a half years of operation, the company has become one of the country's top three suppliers.

Dewji's master plan is to have set up in Kenya, Rwanda, Madagascar, Ethiopia, Burundi, Ghana and Nigeria by 2022, which he believes will increase his workforce from 28000 – about 5 per cent of Tanzania's formal employment – to 100000; the textile arm alone employs 4000 people. Such expansion should secure the revenue of $5 billion per annum that Dewji yearns for MeTL, in which he has a 75 per cent stake, to make.

But two of Dewji's plans don't manifest the same shrewdness as the one above: his decision to invest millions of dollars in a football club and to go head to head with a world giant in fizzy drinks. Many consider these as flights of fancy, and wonder why he would risk it.

'My dream is to have a drinks brand that is bought across the whole of Africa,' Dewji says firmly.

For this to happen, he is willing to risk spectacular and humiliating defeat in an attempt to give Coca-Cola – one of the biggest brand names on earth – one in the eye. Taking on the mighty giant of the fizzy-drink business has proved the graveyard of many a hard-nosed billionaire's ego. Look at British tycoon Richard Branson, who has made a success of almost every business he's touched, from airlines to music. Coca-Cola knocked out his Virgin Cola in the first round.

Dewji believes he can box cleverer than Branson. He has been in the soft-drink and juice business for a while and has the machinery for mass production – plus a good deal of hope. When he launched his cheekily named Mo Cola in Tanzania a couple of years ago – his friends call him Mo – Coca-Cola took notice, even though they hold a whopping 96 per cent market share in Tanzania. Dewji claims that Coca-Cola offered to purchase his bottling plant, but he refused. He is settling in for a long and slow campaign against the American giant, as the fizzy-drink war in Tanzania is likely to be drawn out, which is putting it mildly. Even though Dewji turns out 12 million bottles a month at his three bottling plants in Dar es Salaam, he has managed to capture only 3.5 per cent of the market. Not that it worries this all-or-nothing entrepreneur.

'Once I get to 15 per cent, I will start making money,' he says. His optimism is almost tangible, but his target appears light years away.

An even bigger drain on Dewji's pocket is likely to be Simba Sports Club, one of Tanzania's biggest football teams. He paid $10 million for the down-on-its-uppers team, which he sponsored between 1999 and 2005, in the hope of turning it into one of Africa's richest clubs with the finest players.

'I want to see Simba win the CAF Champions League title,' Dewji says. 'The club, which will celebrate its 80th anniversary on 8 August 2016, is not supposed to be where it is at the moment. Going for four seasons without winning the League is unacceptable.'

As with most of Dewji's business deals, he has thought about his strategy and structured the deal carefully. He plans to invest seed money of 20 billion shillings (US$9 million) for three years into a high-interest account that will earn 17.5 per cent interest and thus help to increase the club's capital. Dewji will also spend millions of dollars to buy new players and construct infrastructure, like a new training ground in Bunju, on the outskirts of Dar es Salaam.

Like the $500 000 Dewji ploughs into his hometown of Singida every year to provide water, food and education to the people of his region, it is money spent with the best of intentions, but it could prove a heavy drain on both the entrepreneur's time and pocket. When South African mining billionaire Patrice Motsepe was asked about his charitable causes, he joked that his football club, Premier Soccer League side Mamelodi Sundowns, was the biggest charity of all.

Wealth is not earned without sacrifice. Every morning, Dewji – who lives with his wife, daughter and two sons in one of Dar es Salaam's most exclusive neighbourhoods – starts work in his office at 6 a.m. He spends the first hour responding to emails and reading commodity reports, and then runs meetings until lunch time.

'People in Tanzania look at my wealth and think I must be sunbathing and playing golf all day. But I work really hard. I put in a hundred hours a week. It's a never-ending game. You can never say, "I've worked hard enough now,"' Dewji says. 'When I feel my energy levels starting to drop, I drive to the gym near my house. Every day, I run three kilometres and lift weights. I like to keep fit.'

After gym, he goes home for lunch and to play with his children for 15 minutes before he returns to the office until late at night. The only days he takes off are Sundays, when he spends time with his family.

'Until about four years ago, I also used to work on Sundays, but my wife almost divorced me!' he jokes.

All that hard work has allowed for a luxurious lifestyle. Dewji can afford to look good, and he enjoys fashion. 'I have a huge wardrobe of suits and over 200 glasses. I like to match the frames with my glasses. I like to match the frames with my suits. At the moment I am not very happy with my brand, because they have stopped distributing colour frames, which means I can only wear black suits.

'You have to live well, but you don't have to live lavishly, to the extreme. You need to be humble. I could buy a plane, a Rolls-Royce or a Bentley. But I don't. If drilling a borehole costs $20 000, you tell me to buy a watch for $20 000? To make a decision that has an impact on people's lives is a one-second decision for me. If you get too egocentric, you lose your vision. It deceives you.'

Not everyone in Tanzania likes the Tsar of Dar. Wealth often generates jealousy; there are those who believe that Dewji does not do enough to support black Tanzanians in his huge operations. With the speed he has made his first billion, in just over a decade, he has probably managed to step on a number of powerful toes along the way.

Many also questioned his dual roles as a Member of Parliament for Singida, with all the political influence that job carried, and an entrepreneur. Dewji gave up his seat in 2015, after occupying it for 10 years, and told me that he had always been a reluctant politician – the job gave him grey hairs. He was definitely an entrepreneur first and a politician second.

In July 2016, Dewji signed the Giving Pledge, founded by billionaires Warren Buffett and Bill Gates, according to which he agreed to give away at least half of his wealth.

'Having witnessed severe poverty throughout my upbringing, I have always felt a deep responsibility to give back to my community,' he says in the letter that confirmed his pledge. 'I am very conscious of everything I do. If you get too engrossed in making money, you lose focus on life. Life is very short. I don't want to die with all this money.'

For now, Dewji appears to have a firm grip on both his ego and his ability to make millions.

4

The $600-million-a-year rent collector

Sudhir Ruparelia

Sudhir Ruparelia

I T WAS ONE of those tranquil scenes you could take to the grave. The morning sun cast dappled shadows over the mass of pink and orange bougainvillea growing over the patio at the Kabira Country Club in Kampala, the capital of Uganda. It was already warm; there was not a breath of wind. Over the tables buzzed scores of large moths; everyone agreed that there were more than usual, which they attributed to the sudden transition from the heat of summer to the rainy season. Quick-stepping, uniformed waiters bearing coffee did the rounds. This was the scene for breakfast with a billionaire who once upon a time drove a taxi and worked in a supermarket. He now owned the country club.

It may have been just another Thursday morning in Uganda, but on a beautiful day like this, life appears to be laid out at your feet, as bright as the sun. What a day to shoot the breeze with one of Africa's handful of billionaires! Such encounters are rare on this continent – most of Africa's wealthiest people are reluctant to meet with anyone not interested in doing a deal. So, in more ways than one, this meeting in Kampala was one for the book.

Across the table from me sat Sudhir Ruparelia, one of Uganda's few dollar billionaires, and the first Ugandan to appear on the cover of *Forbes Africa*. A great bear of a man, with more white hairs than me, he was about a million miles from the London buses on which he would travel to work to grind out a living.

Ruparelia is a remarkable entrepreneur. He turned a mere $25 000 into a personal fortune of $1.1 billion in less than 30 years, according to *Forbes*. In 2016, this fortune has shrunk, slightly, to $800 million, but he is still the 27th richest person in Africa. No mean feat when you consider that the man fled his country for a foreign land with nothing to his name – no silver spoon, no family firm ... not even a wealthy uncle to guide him.

After years of talking to the super-rich, I have a theory that money and manners are inversely proportional. I can attest that Ruparelia – even though he enjoys the occasional affectation of smoking expensive cigars – is the exception to the rule. He is nothing if not down to earth, a man comfortable in his own skin, who appears to face the vagaries of life with a chuckle. In this, maybe, we are kindred spirits.

People in Kampala say he is a tough businessman, with a razor-keen eye for deals, and that he takes no prisoners. Although that might be true, he also displays a healthy dose of humility, frequently mentioning his humble beginnings. However, you ignore the steely glint in his eye at your own peril. It warns you that you would last about as long as a snowflake in summer if you opposed him in any business deal he was orchestrating.

Sudhir Ruparelia took an unconventional path to wealth. There are no money markets, sharp suits or clever investments in his remarkable story, which began when he was forced to flee Uganda more than 40 years ago.

It was the worst of times for Uganda when President Idi Amin, who assumed power in a coup in 1971, ordered 60 000 of the so-called Ugandan Asians to leave the country by August 1972. Amin's intention was to transfer economic control of Uganda into the hands of Ugandans, a move that was to prove catastrophic for the country's economy.

Amin's decree resulted in a mad scramble for the airport. Mobs assaulted the fleeing Ugandan Asians and, in the months that followed, the bodies of those who didn't manage to escape were found floating in the local rivers.

Ruparelia was young and right in the thick of the melee. He knew the dangers, but, like many teenagers, he thought he was indestructible. And besides, his family had lived in Africa for generations, for the best part of a century.

Originally from India, the Ruparelia family had landed in Mombasa, Kenya, in 1897, where they set up a trading store. They moved to Uganda in 1903. For years, Ruparelia's family had run a shop and petrol station in Queen Elizabeth National Park, in the west of Uganda. As 1972 slipped away, so did most of the family. They threw themselves upon the mercy of the British government and ended up in London, one of the few places in the world where they could run, as many held British passports.

Ruparelia, however, who had just turned 16 and was as fearless as any youngster, told his family he wasn't going anywhere. He saw his parents off at the airport and agreed to follow them later, as long as they left him enough money to survive. They did, and the teenager spent it in the raucous bars and nightclubs of the capital. He was having the time of his life in Uganda's darkest days.

'We had a lot of money to party and drink,' he recalls more than four decades later.

'The security personnel occasionally stopped us, but we always sweet-talked them into releasing us.'

As the months went by, the political situation got increasingly serious, and the sweet-talk lost its effect. On the day one of his friends was arrested by security men, Ruparelia decided to flee Kampala.

'The city was getting desolate. There were only around 100 Asians left,' he says.

He boarded a plane as quickly as he could and landed in London, with no idea where his family was – Facebook or Google Maps did not exist in those days. Like most of the Asian exiles from Uganda, he was sent to a refugee camp. But he couldn't stand it there and left after just one day, to find friends he had heard were living not far away, in Finchley Central in North London. He found eight of them living in a two-roomed house and became resident number nine.

The young man needed money, and fast, to survive on the tough streets of London. He talked his way into a job where he earned $30 a week, at a supermarket in Golders Green, North London.

'Hey, that was good money then!' he counters when I chuckle at the image of Uganda's richest man pushing trollies and stacking shelves.

Years of menial jobs and working for a pittance followed. Ruparelia is probably one of the few dollar billionaires in the world who once pulled doughnuts at dawn out of a spitting hot-fat fryer in a cake shop and injected them with jam – a rare skill.

'It is very difficult to do. You have to take the doughnut out of the hot fat and inject it with jam in one movement, before it goes cold. If you get it wrong, it is very easy to get burnt by the fat,' he remembers.

Another hard, poorly paid job was to pour hot wax to burn measuring tables into laboratory test tubes. It was one of three jobs he held down at the same time to make ends meet.

'When you have done these menial tasks, you know what life is all about.'

With a few pounds in his pocket, Ruparelia could finally set out to find his parents in the expatriate Asian community.

'You couldn't just ring people up or email them in those days,' he laughs.

His search ended in the windswept seaside town of Scunthorpe on England's east coast. We both laugh when he tells me, 'I'm afraid you have to have lived in England to get the joke, but in those days [Scunthorpe] was unfashionable and one of the last places on earth you would expect to find anyone, let alone refugees from Uganda.'

Reunited with his family, Ruparelia could finally concentrate on looking for a decent job. There were some disappointments along the way. He was turned down for a job at the Ford car factory because it was a union-closed shop and he wasn't a member; and he was denied the chance to become an airman in the Royal Air Force, despite passing the tests, because he was a minor and his mother refused to sign the consent forms. The violent turmoil in Uganda had turned her against the military for life.

However, at least some good fortune befell Ruparelia as he scraped by in London. He spotted his future wife, Jyotsna, through the top window of a double-decker bus on his way home one night along London's grey streets. Luckily, his friend sitting next to him knew the young lady's family and arranged a meeting, which paved the way for nearly 40 years of marriage.

Jyotsna, who would later become a banker, encouraged her future husband to concentrate on one business. This simple piece of advice was the gateway to Ruparelia's fortune.

When the two married, they decided to venture into the London property market. The couple bought houses, renovated them and sold them at a profit. The early 1980s was a boom time in property. Margaret Thatcher's free-market economy was at its peak; you could renovate even a garage and sell it for thousands of pounds. People who had previously only been able to rent their council houses were now allowed to buy them, and thousands of them flooded onto the property market. It created a housing boom, and Ruparelia made a fortune from it.

In 1985, his relatives in Uganda advised him that it was safe to come home.

'When Africa is in your blood, you will always come back,' he says.

He took the $25 000 he'd made from his London property deals and flew home. But just when he thought it was safe to get back in the water, there were two military coups in six months, which brought the tanks back onto the streets of Kampala. Ruparelia could have been forgiven if he'd headed straight back to the airport, but he didn't.

In the first coup, General Tito Okello ousted President Milton Obote to install himself as president, on 27 July 1985. The current president, Yoweri Museveni, ousted Okello six months later.

Ruparelia, understandably, kept a low profile in his first year back on home turf. It allowed him the time to study what was left of the economy. He saw two opportunities amid all the chaos.

'In Africa, feasibility studies are a waste of time. It is about the ability to see opportunity and take it on. If you did feasibility studies for a country like Uganda, you would never do anything.'

Firstly, he spotted that the Ugandan economy was being hit by a foreign-exchange shortage at a time when the Ugandan shilling (Ush) had dropped to a low of Ush600 to the dollar. Secondly, the civil war had left the breweries in ruins. Reasoning that people always found money for beer, Ruparelia opened a wholesale store in December 1986 in downtown Kampala, which sold beer, salt and wine. He positioned himself as a conduit between importers and retailers, setting up a solid distribution structure in Kampala that imported beer with shipments of household goods and got the stock to retailers, on time, at a price they could afford.

Over time, he became a trusted business partner of the importers, who supplied him on credit and claimed their money only after a few days.

'While in London, the strongest trait I'd learnt was to be disciplined. I ensured that the suppliers' money was always readily available, as agreed,' he reflects.

It took just three months, but numerous shipments, for him to become the biggest dealer in imported beer in Kampala. With the supply network in place, Ruparelia worked hard to elevate himself to importer. For this, he needed piles of foreign currency, so he started up a currency exchange service, another vast, untapped market in Uganda.

The business went off like a rocket. Demand for hard currency was so strong that the business was making $10 000 a day, Ruparelia says. Using the experience he'd gained in London, he invested this money in prime properties in Kampala.

When the government moved in to regulate the mushrooming currency business in 1990, Ruparelia's Crane Forex Bureau became the first in the country to be licensed. This catapulted his business beyond his wildest dreams. In just six months, according to him, he was making more money than established commercial banks. It encouraged him to expand his financial services empire.

Ruparelia believed that the commercial banks were complacent, operating as if they were doing people a favour by dealing with them. Also, bank charges were high and the choices limited. In 1995, he took on the established commercial banks when he launched Crane Bank with a million dollars. His approach was simple: lower the bank charges, cut the red tape, provide longer banking hours, and open on Saturdays. One has to wonder why banks around the world do not open at weekends when their customers can use them, rather than keep them open all week when people are at work.

The strategy was immediately successful. Today, Crane Bank, the second largest commercial bank in Uganda, is worth more than $120 million and has 38 branches across the country. It was voted Bank of the Year in Uganda in 2009 and won the Banker of the Year award in 2003, 2005, 2006, 2007 and 2008 from the *Financial Times* in London – the city where Ruparelia had once juggled hot jam doughnuts.

By 2011, the bank** had posted a 32.3 per cent increment in profit, before tax, of $37 million. At the time he was interviewed, Ruparelia attributed its rapid success in an era of banking collapses to its strategy of opening at least 10 new branches a year. 'There are currently about 35 million people in Uganda; only three and a half million people live in Kampala. The rest of the population is in the countryside. That has guided our philosophy of opening more branches upcountry.'

The plan then was to expand into South Sudan and Rwanda, the latter a country on a remarkable rise since it was torn apart by genocide 20 years ago. Rwanda has orchestrated an incredible high-tech economic revival that would have done post-war Germany, or Japan, proud.

Ruparelia felt that Rwanda's revival had created a new generation of middle-class shoppers and the promise of brisk business. For that reason, he would be building a shopping mall on the site of a demolished police barracks in the centre of Kigali. Part of the mall will be a bus station, where hordes of shoppers from across the country can disgorge into a variety of shops – a classic case of an entrepreneur who spots an opportunity and takes a risk.

On the other hand, experts say that setting up and sustaining a business in Ruparelia's heartland of Kampala is not easy. Augustus Nuwagaba, an economics professor at Makerere University in Kampala, says, 'Sudhir started small a couple of decades back. If he hadn't kept the discipline, his efforts would have collapsed at the incubation stage, like many businesses in this country do.'

---

* Crane Bank went into receivership in 2016 and is currently licensed and supervised by the Bank of Uganda, the central bank and national banking regulator. *Forbes Africa* will be conducting a follow-up interview with Sudhir Ruparelia in 2017.

Nuwagaba dismisses those who envy Sudhir Ruparelia and his fortune.

'We would be totally unjust not to commend people who make it from scratch. The opportunities are available to everybody. It is the application of the underlying business principles that makes the difference.'

Paul Busharizi, a respected business journalist in Kampala, compares Ruparelia to Africa's richest man, Aliko Dangote of Nigeria. 'While the rest of us are paralysed by problems, these billionaires focus on how to overcome them. But it starts in the mind … There are hundreds of real estate brokers and developers, forex bureau owners and flower farmers doing the same thing that Sudhir does, but they are not as rich. The difference has to be their visions.'

Like Nuwagaba, Busharizi dismisses Ruparelia's detractors in Kampala and commends him for investing nine out of every 10 shillings he earns in property. 'The more people you serve, the more money you make. We might begrudge men like Sudhir for their billions, but we are the ones who willingly fork [the money] over to pay for the services he delivers to us.'

The real estate business has by far been the biggest money spinner for Ruparelia. Year after year, he has sunk nine shillings out of every 10 into bricks and mortar. His property company is called Meera Investments, after his eldest daughter, a sign of how close he is to his family. Meera Investments owns more than 300 residential and commercial properties, from the massive Crane Chambers in downtown Kampala to scores of office blocks, shopping malls, apartments and tracts of land. Ruparelia estimates that the company collects more than $600 million a year in rent.

In January 2016, Ruparelia opened the $25-million Hardware City in Kampala, which sells exactly what you think it does. Tenants are lured by the bait that rent is paid in Ugandan shillings rather than dollars, with no increase for two years.

The jewel in Ruparelia's real estate crown is the five-star Speke Resort, built on 75 acres on the shores of Lake Victoria in Kampala. The hotel consists of 780 rooms, a 1 000-seat ballroom and Uganda's only Olympic-size swimming pool.

The plush resort, worth around $165 million, made headlines when it caught the eye of Libyan leader Muammar Gaddafi, who offered $120 million for it. But Ruparelia, despite several entreaties from his camp, turned Gaddafi down – probably one of only a handful of people who had ever done so. One of Ruparelia's most notable characteristics is that he knows exactly what his assets are worth, and you won't get them for a penny less.

In recent years, Ruparelia has also acquired an education portfolio. He bought Victoria University in Kampala from international education outfit Edulink to add to Kampala International School Uganda and Kampala Parents' School. Together, they are worth an estimated $40 million.

So what next for the billionaire of Uganda, who already owns a large slice of his country and is wealthy beyond most people's dreams? Ruparelia's face lights up when he talks about roses. He is very proud of his efforts to grow these flowers in the wetlands of Entebbe, on the shores of Lake Victoria, where the kind and temperate climate allows them to grow all year round. It is his pet project, and he hopes it will be a big part of his legacy as an entrepreneur. Rosebud Ltd has exported millions of stems to Holland and Germany, Europe's biggest rose markets, and in the process Ruparelia has captured 40 per cent of Uganda's flower-export market.

'The Dutch are tough, but when they say they will pay, they pay,' he chuckles.

The greenhouses on the farm cover a total of 50 hectares, and produce and export over 13 million stems per month, earning Ruparelia $5 million in profit every year. True to form, he is thinking about expanding the business, increasing the greenhouses to cover 200 hectares in the hope of producing half a million roses a day. This expansion will create 7 000 jobs and generate revenue of up to $100 million.

It is ironic that this business, which gives Ruparelia such pleasure, also gave him his biggest headache, when the National Association of Professional Environmentalists accused Rosebud of polluting the Lutembe wetlands with pesticide and fertiliser effluent. The Ugandan parliamentary committee on natural resources launched an inquiry, but the Speaker of the House halted proceedings, declaring the matter sub judice.

In 2013, people living near the rose farm tried to block the access roads in protest against its expansion. Ruparelia's lawyers sought a court injunction to continue with the development, but he is reluctant to say more except that his plans have the blessing of the environmental regulator.

The National Environment Management Authority, a semi-autonomous institution that regulates environmental matters in Uganda, has cleared Rosebud of any wrongdoing.

Its executive director, Tom Okia Okurut, said in 2014: 'We licensed Rosebud in 2004 with well-stipulated guidelines to follow in safeguarding the environment. We have been monitoring their operations and have no queries save for the wrong perceptions of some members of the public.'

Africa is likely to hear more of Ruparelia, a man who has shown African entrepreneurs what calculated risk, a little humility, disciplined investment and a good deal of hard work can do. He is in the process of building a multimillion-dollar home in North London, not too far from the supermarkets and cake shops of his youth. It is an unspoken victory for an African who proves that it doesn't matter who you are or how dire your circumstances – if you take a risk and work hard, you can make it.

It is surely one of the great ironies of Africa that none of this may have happened were it not for a demented leader like President Idi Amin.

5

The Capitalist Crusader

Herman Mashaba

Herman Mashaba

WHEN YOU ARE rich and well known, you make enemies; if you are rich, well known and in politics, you make even more enemies, faster.

It was a strange decision, to say the least, especially since millionaire Herman Mashaba had said, in a *Forbes Africa* article, that he would never go into politics.

'There's no way you are going to see me toyi-toying,' he had told *Forbes Africa*. 'I've never toyi-toyied in my 56 years of living, so I don't think I will start now. I think I will be a stupid politician. If there was no Democratic Alliance, there would be no one I would vote for. Yes, they are not perfect, but they represent my value system.'

But then Mashaba took the political plunge in 2016, risking a lifetime's vilification on social media. His choice of party made it even worse – he chose to stand as the mayoral candidate for Johannesburg, a cash-strapped African city groaning under the strain of a growing population, for the opposition Democratic Alliance (DA) party.

'I am not scared,' he says on a summer's afternoon in his well-appointed, secluded mansion in Sandton, the business district of Johannesburg. Mashaba gets very animated when he talks. He gestures vigorously with his hands and hits the table in time with the words he wants to emphasise.

Mashaba was born in 1959, at the height of apartheid South Africa, which makes his choice of political party even harder for some people to accept. Many of his peers view the DA as a 'white' party of privilege; ergo, any influential black man who throws in his lot with South Africa's official opposition is pretty much a sell-out.

'I could no longer ignore the call to help my country,' Mashaba says earnestly. He adds that he isn't worried about what people think of him. Just as well.

Mashaba says that he had resolved to step forward in December 2015, when President Jacob Zuma fired his finance minister, Nhlanhla Nene, in a shock move. Zuma had then appointed rookie David van Rooyen in Nene's place, before being persuaded to call back previous incumbent Pravin Gordhan days later. Three finance ministers in four days sent the rand and the markets plummeting, costing the economy millions of rands.

'I feared for the future of my country,' Mashaba says.

Against seemingly overwhelming odds, the ruling ANC lost its majority in Johannesburg in the August 2016 municipal elections, and Mashaba was elected mayor at the city council's first sitting on a pro-business and anti-corruption ticket. The anti-capitalist, red-beret-wearing Economic Freedom Fighters (EFF) had agreed to vote with the DA, and contributed 10 per cent of the votes needed for the party to take power in Johannesburg.

It is an uneasy alliance, to say the least, Mashaba admits. But it helped put him in charge of a budget of R55 billion (bigger than that of a few small countries) and 33 000 employees, serving nearly five million people. Assuming power over a city like Jozi was not as simple as it might have seemed on the day Mashaba was elected mayor. For a start, the city's budget had been set weeks before he took over, which means that for most of his first year in office, Mashaba must work with money that had been allocated by his predecessors, who are also his political opponents.

'Everyone is saying we want to see changes now, but it is very difficult, because it is not my budget. My hands are tied,' Mashaba admits.

There is a heap of files on Mashaba's desk, many of them penned by the auditors KPMG. These are the result of his earlier crusade against corruption.

'This is somewhere I can make a difference,' Mashaba says, shuffling the files with relish.

Mashaba claims that the files contain clear-cut cases of corruption perpetrated in the City of Johannesburg. These include scams that purloined millions in hard-earned cash from the city's residents. On this day in December, Mashaba claims that arrest warrants have been issued, and that up to 160 people, many of them top city managers, could be arrested. As we speak, he is trying to persuade the National Prosecuting Authority (NPA) to act on the cases, which is likely to cause a huge uproar.

'I want to get people locked up to show that we will no longer allow the money of the people to be looted in this fashion,' Mashaba says, warming to his theme. 'Where I grew up, in a small, poor township, everyone was stealing; everyone spoke openly about stealing opportunities, because we had nothing. We even had to steal water from a nearby farmer because we had no running water. These days you have wealthy people in positions of power stealing millions every year – for what? This must be stopped, and this is where we begin to stop it.'

Mashaba also says he is pushing ahead with his plans for a skills audit in the City of Johannesburg to ensure that the right people are in the right jobs; this in an attempt to clear away the crony system and get rid of the incompetent and any political appointees. But it is easier said than done. Mashaba has already taken flak from his senior managers after an incident when he sat staff down, many of them women in senior jobs, to share his vision of a corruption-free future in all appointments.

After the meeting, a complaint was lodged at the mayor's office, accusing him of inferring that his female managers were like prostitutes who had slept their way to the top. The story travelled far and wide across Johannesburg. Mashaba is taking it up with his lawyers.

'All I said was that we are a professional organisation and that [we are] not going to employ fathers, friends, wives and girlfriends. I made that statement and I am not going to apologise. What has that got to do with prostitutes?'

One point, however, is clear, and that is that Mashaba has the devil's own job. For the man who outwitted apartheid laws to make his fortune, this may be his toughest challenge yet.

Herman Mashaba was born into poverty in rural South Africa, but he managed to claw his way up to fame and a considerable fortune by fighting the odds, rising to every challenge that came his way, and bending the rules to fit his needs.

When Mashaba appeared on the cover of *Forbes Africa* in 2012, a time when many black South Africans were propagating national-isation and socialism, we called him the Capitalist Crusader. He was so proud of that title, he named his next book after it. It speaks volumes about the confidence of the man and his aspirations.

'I want to be known as a capitalist,' Mashaba says. 'I wrote the book openly, so that people will know my agenda upfront. At the same time, I don't want to be misrepresented. Unfortunately, collective thinking to a large extent misleads people. Most people's agendas are not what they preach. Let's judge each other on the basis of what we are doing, not what we are preaching.

'We have a crisis on our hands, and we have to address it now. When we fought apartheid, it was not to replace it with something worse. Capitalism has become something of a dirty word, while the unions and the youth wing of the ruling party are free to talk socialism.'

Apartheid was a harsh reality among poor black South Africans when Mashaba was born in Hammanskraal, north of Pretoria, in 1959. He was two years old when his father died, leaving his domestic-worker mother to raise the boy and his four sisters alone. She worked for a white family in the exclusive suburb of Sandton, not too far from where Mashaba's luxury home stands today. She wasn't allowed out in the evenings. If she wanted to see her children, she had to sneak out, take a train to Hammanskraal and get back before dawn. Often, she could only visit once a month.

As Mashaba grew up, he watched other boys go in search of week-end jobs in the gardens of the white suburbs of Pretoria North. The indignities these boys suffered for a few coins and the stories they relayed to their peers were too much for the young Mashaba to bear. The risk he took in response says a lot about the man and his approach to entrepreneurship.

Mashaba decided to become a 'knocksman', someone who runs a backstreet dice game. It is a very dangerous occupation – the punters drink alcohol and carry knives; they can get angry and violent if they lose, or if the knocksman wants to pack up and go home with his winnings. But the 'job' not only supplied the money Mashaba needed; he also relished the risk, seeing life as a game of chance.

Mashaba's first customers were his friends, those who worked in the gardens of Pretoria North. He argued that if he was prepared to risk ending up in hospital with a knife wound to provide a service, it didn't matter that he was taking money from his friends, who could ill afford to lose it. No risk, no reward – an attitude that would prevail in the boardrooms he would later frequent.

The dice paid his way through high school, whereas before he had struggled to raise 25 cents in school fees. He matriculated in 1979 and attained a place at the University of the North, in Turfloop, Limpopo, for a Bachelor of Administration degree, majoring in political science and public administration. He wanted to study law, but because he had failed Afrikaans, which, at the time, was a prerequisite and a subject he didn't really take to, he failed to qualify.

These were turbulent times at the University of the North. In the apartheid years, this university was one of five that authorities referred to as 'bush universities'. They were smaller, poorer and had narrower curriculums than those of white universities, and catered for a small group of black students, hand-picked by the authorities, from families where at least one parent was formally employed, usually as a nurse, teacher, preacher or policeman. The education centred around rote learning, where facts were to be memorised and regurgitated.

It was an unintended consequence of the system that these universities became cauldrons of political unrest and activism. Some of the student activists at the University of the North would become household names in the cause of the struggle: current deputy president Cyril Ramaphosa, Frank Chikane and Barney Pityana, among others.

The simmering discontent among the students signalled the end of Mashaba's short university career. In 1980, in his second year, campus unrest forced the authorities to shut down the university and send the students home. To this day, Mashaba has never returned to his alma mater.

'One day we were ordered by police to leave the university immediately. I never understood why they had to involve law enforcement in solving matters with the students. I simply packed my bags and went home,' Mashaba recalls wistfully 40 years later.

Back home, life was hard. Mashaba has never tried to airbrush his past as so many of the rich and famous are wont to do, which attests to his integrity. He has admitted that he both smoked and sold marijuana when he was a youth in Hammanskraal, and that he stole. Once, he illegally appropriated a welding machine and buried it until he could find a buyer. When he found out what the machine was for, he sold it to the township gangster.

Every day, Mashaba was forced to take risks to put food on the table. In his dealing days, transporting marijuana into Hammanskraal, he recalls feeling sick with fear whenever he came upon a police roadblock, knowing that discovery would result in being locked up for years.

He also endured some frustrating months during which he tried to leave the country to join an exiled liberation movement, but he never succeeded. Instead, he decided to look for a job. He found one in a supermarket, as a despatch clerk, and he worked there for seven months before starting at a furniture store. More than two years later, bored and frustrated, he spotted a classified advertisement in a newspaper seeking sales representatives. You can write your own pay cheque, the ad said; all you needed was a car and some selling experience.

Mashaba had never driven a car, let alone owned one. Within two months he had not only arranged for driving lessons, but had bought a car on hire purchase ... and got married. The marriage was a deliberate move on his part. He thought that settling down would keep him from being distracted from his mission of becoming an entrepreneur. He and his wife, Connie Mashaba – who now runs the family investments, while he runs the city – have been together ever since and have two children.

The job where you could 'write your own pay cheque' proved not so straightforward. Every day, for years, Mashaba had to defy the strict apartheid pass laws that prevented black people from 'loitering' in white surburbia. If you got caught by the police, you could be beaten up or spend a couple of days in the cells, or both, with no recourse. After all that, you could also face the sack.

But with his legendary appetite for risk, Mashaba relentlessly knocked on doors in the streets where he is now mayor. He faced vicious guard dogs and racist tirades from the residents, but once he got through the gate, he charmed his customers into buying everything from dinner sets to linen, crockery, fire-detection equipment and hair-care products.

It was hard, soul-destroying work, but Mashaba, with his easy manner and ready smile, persevered. Slowly, steadily, the promise that he would write his own handsome pay cheque was fulfilled. Soon he was making two to three times more than black doctors, who were among the best-paid black professionals in South Africa at the time.

But his big break was yet to come. One of the crazes among black South Africans in the 1980s was permed hair; it was the cool fashion statement of the townships and everyone's chance to look like Michael Jackson.

Hair salons mushroomed across the country to cash in on the craze, and Mashaba jumped in too. Selling hair products for permed hair, he earned around R4 000 a month, which, he says, was serious money back then. His contemporaries were earning a few hundred, if they were lucky.

In 1984, while still a salesman, Mashaba was hungry for more and approached two of his colleagues, Joseph Molwantwa, a fellow salesman with whom he grew up, and Johan Kriel, an Afrikaner and production manager who manufactured hair-care products. Mashaba didn't know Kriel well, but he did know that Kriel had run a business that had subsequently failed. However, Mashaba felt Kriel had the precious technical know-how for what Mashaba required. The political situation in the country made it difficult for the two to work together, but Mashaba, as was his wont, pushed on with the kind of raw instinct that would cement his fortune.

'I took a chance and shared my dream with [Kriel],' he recalls with a smile.

It was a move that would make Mashaba a fortune and that led to the creation of South Africa's first black-owned hair-products-manufacturing company. It would soon be famous across the continent.

The unlikely trio approached a township entrepreneur, Walter Dube, for finance. Dube, whose wife was a client of Mashaba's and owned a hair salon, agreed to lend the business R30 000 – a fortune back then. Dube charged them prime plus 10 per cent and insisted on owning 25 per cent of the business. There were few other offers of finance for black entrepreneurs in those days, so everyone agreed and got down to work.

On 14 February 1985, the Black Like Me range of hair products hit the market. Black South Africans fell in love with the products, which promised perfect curls. Soon every salon in the township had a bottle: a black-owned, black-manufactured hair product that was tailor-made for black hair.

Mashaba, Molwantwa, Kriel and the money man, Dube, reaped rich and rapid rewards as people everywhere permed their hair. They exported the products to neighbouring countries, and the Black Like Me name spread quickly. They repaid Dube's loan within seven months.

Four years later, Mashaba bought his friend Molwantwa out. Three years later, he bought out Kriel. Dube cashed in during 1997, when Mashaba decided to sell a 75 per cent majority stake to a multinational, Colgate-Palmolive, hoping that the giant would take the brand further. Alas, he says, it was not to be.

'Slowness, bureaucracy, stood in the way. I quickly made an offer to buy it back,' says Mashaba.

Two years later, Black Like Me was in his hands once again after he had bought it back for much less than he had sold it for.

'Yes, I made another profit,' he admits with a mischievous smile, followed by a chuckle.

Another couple of years later, the company grew by 47 per cent after Mashaba rebranded it, launched it in more countries, including the United Kingdom, and added fragrances and cosmetics to his range.

But not everything had been plain sailing. In 1993, Mashaba had built a R10-million ($725 000) factory in the heart of Mabopane township, north of Pretoria, from the seed capital of R30 000 (around $2 000). One reason why it was located there was that apartheid laws prevented Mashaba from buying or renting land in an industrial area, so he was forced to build his 6 000-square-metre factory in the township.

But obviously Mashaba was too successful for his own good. Black Like Me was thriving and money was being made hand over fist. But someone clearly didn't like this, and they decided to do something about it. It could not have come at a worse time ...

It was a summer's day and the December shopping season was just around the corner, when orders for hair products would increase dramatically. Mashaba was ready for a handsome payday; he planned a 24-hour shift to manufacture as much hair product as possible to meet the increasing demand. Then it all went up in smoke.

'The 17th of November 1993 is a day I will never forget,' he says. 'It's a day I have difficulty explaining, but out of it came a lot of lessons. The incident itself was horrific; how I survived was a miracle. Only God knows.'

It was the worst day of Mashaba's life – a raging fire that had been set in the factory destroyed seven years of hard work within just a few hours.

'I stood there watching the firefighters battling the fire in my factory. I immediately realised it was not an accidental fire; it was spread across the factory. When the fire department combed the place, they found evidence of an arsonist. Unfortunately, when the workers started to arrive for the six o'clock shift, the factory was in ashes. You can imagine, R10 million in 1993 is close to R100 million today. More than 150 people were crying for their jobs,' Mashaba remembers.

But there was no time for tears, he says. His suppliers' trucks arrived to deliver stock to the burnt-down factory, and he had to find alternative storerooms. By 9 a.m., he had assembled his management team to discuss an alternative venue. Within two weeks, he had found a smaller factory in Midrand, between Pretoria and Johannesburg. But it took two years to get back to full production at a time of intense competition.

'The lesson for me was that while I went through this, people moved on. That's where I lost market share. The products were not on the shelves,' Mashaba says.

Despite asking people for information and offering a R50 000 ($3 600) reward, no one was ever prosecuted for burning down his factory.

Mashaba credits his culture of saving for getting him back on his feet. When the insurance company took a long time to pay up, Mashaba used his savings to purchase the new factory in Midrand.

'I didn't even get half of what I was insured for, and they took time to pay me out. You can imagine the banks at the time – as blacks, they were not interested in us. The only relationship I had with banks was to deposit my money,' he says. 'Fortunately, I never allowed circumstances to determine my fate. I have always believed I was in control of my destiny. I don't want politicians', or anyone's, favours.'

The following year could have been as lucrative for Mashaba as 1993 had been disastrous. The newly elected ANC government had adopted Black Economic Empowerment (BEE) as their official policy to uplift the previously disadvantaged and to empower black business. According to the legislation, white-owned companies had to bring black shareholders on board by giving them equity if they wanted to stay in business.

'I wasn't initially attracted to BEE when it started,' Mashaba says. 'It made no sense to me, even though I had invitations. But as soon as it dawned on me that this thing is happening with or without me, I decided to take advantage.'

It may have taken a few years for Mashaba to dip in his toe, but take advantage he did. In 2002 he became part of a consortium that bought 10 per cent of a ferrochrome smelter from Samancor, a South African chrome-producing company that supplies nearly a third of the world's demand. A few years later, the consortium increased its stake to 19.9 per cent. Keen to demonstrate that he always makes money, Mashaba points out that he spent R40 million on the Samancor deal and sold his stake for R2 billion a few years later. And he bought Stocks Building Africa for R80 million and sold it for R1.1 billion a couple of years ago.

More than a decade down the line and Mashaba has built his own investment vehicle, a fairly low-key affair as far as multimillion-dollar investment companies go. Lephatsi Investments is run from a tiny office in Sandton with only a handful of staff. However, it manages more than R600 million in assets and has stakes in 12 different listed and non-listed companies that operate across the mining and energy industries, and in property management and information-communication technology.

So, considering the fact that a great majority of South Africans can't even dream of, let alone own, such vast amounts of money, doesn't Mashaba think it's a bit unfair to expect workers to agree to less generous working conditions without the protection of the law? I am, of course, referring to the fact that Mashaba had challenged the Labour Relations Act – the cornerstone of post-apartheid labour legislation that protects workers' rights – in the Constitutional Court, the highest court in South Africa. According to him, the Act is too inflexible and deters entrepreneurs from hiring people whom they may struggle to fire if they fail to do their job.

'No,' Mashaba says in answer to my question. 'Never take away from people the opportunity to make money. Let's make policies to ensure that we are fair. Let's make sure we manage the greed. But let's allow South Africans to be natural. My understanding of the capitalist system is that it's only natural. It's a natural system for human beings.'

Mashaba's critics claimed that by challenging the Act, he was compromising the welfare of the impoverished people from which he came. Even to suggest that the labour laws should be repealed had in the past drawn severe criticism from the two-million strong Congress of South African Trade Unions (COSATU), which threatened 'blood on the floor'.

In 2012, Sdumo Dlamini, the then president of COSATU, said: 'If anything, COSATU wants the Labour Relations Act tightened. We want to remind Mashaba that even the current arrangement was negotiated.'

The closest big business had ever come to challenging the legislation was to declare it restrictive and suggest that it should perhaps be reviewed. No one had ever dared to oppose it as vehemently as Mashaba, who was backed by two prominent law firms that offered him free legal advice. Mashaba commissioned a report he could put before the courts.

He explains his viewpoint: 'This higher unemployment of South African people is a man-made phenomenon created by the government. It seems to be in our government's interest for people not to work, so that they depend on government grants. If they really wanted people to work, they would create an environment for entrepreneurs and capitalists to create work for people. We need a free market. They must ask their colleagues in China and Russia what communism did to people.

'To protect democracy, you need active citizenship; you don't need to be politicians. If South Africa wants to be a model and a prosperous nation, we need a free-market system. You cannot prosper if the government is the driver of the economy. Just create the environment that will allow the ±50-million South Africans to be the players. And the sooner we abolish all race-based legislation, the better for the future of this country. It is very dangerous to run the country on the basis of race and tribalism.'

In the ensuing years, Mashaba's case ran out of steam because of a lack of money. By then his face was on the DA's election posters and, not too long after that, he was settling into the mayor's chair.

Entering politics is another huge risk for Mashaba, and before the elections many analysts had claimed that he didn't have a hope in hell, but he has proven them wrong – at least in the short term. It seems the spirit of the old knocksman couldn't resist another roll of the dice.

'Yes, you are right,' Mashaba nods, 'being a knocksman was good preparation for running things. People wanted to play my dice games because they knew I was fair and stuck to the rules. People want to play a game with a strong knocksman who enforces the rules and doesn't sit on the fence. You have to say one plus one is two and it will never be three! You always have to play by the rules.'

Many political careers end in failure. If it all falls apart for Mashaba in his guise as a politician, he can always go back to being an entrepreneur. Because one thing is certain: come hell or high water, he *will* make money.

6

Oh, lucky man!: Tim Tebeila, mining millionaire and barefoot dreamer

Tim Tebeila

Tim Tebeila

I T WASN'T THE kind of call you'd expect from a mining millionaire. One night, as I was driving home, my phone rang. It's not unusual for me to field calls at odd times – it is the price of being an editor.

'Chris, it is about time I appeared on your cover,' Tim Tebeila said with a chuckle. He must have been babysitting at home, because I could hear a number of small children talking and crying in the background; one of them sounded like he or she was on Tebeila's lap.

I often get this sort of call, but they are normally from highly paid public relations people who are keen to dazzle you with their employer's wisdom and achievements. It is much like someone trying to sell car insurance and about as engaging.

But this personal plea appeared more vulnerable and from the heart, and it seemed to deserve a hearing. I tactfully explained to Mr Tebeila that to even be considered for the cover of *Forbes Africa*, the minimum net worth of an entrepreneur would have to run into hundreds of millions of US dollars. And he would have to allow one of our journalists to sift through his books and estimate his net worth.

At this point, a lot of entrepreneurs usually take flight for fear of the taxman or other concerns, but Tebeila agreed graciously. In time, we calculated his wealth at a 'mere' $28 million dollars. It was not too shabby for a man who had grown up in grinding poverty. With his wealth established, we told Tebeila that we would happily feature him inside the magazine, but he would not appear on the cover. He graciously accepted the offer, as well as the fact that he had not yet made it, but he vowed to be on the cover one day.

It is Tebeila's humility, laced with a strong dose of ambition, which propelled the barefoot boy from the rocky mountains of Limpopo, in northern South Africa, to a comfy seat at the head of the boardroom table. His mining company has made him more money than he could ever have dreamt of in his youth.

For Tebeila, it was a long walk from his poor childhood to fame and fortune. In Africa, people would say Tebeila was cooked and boiled, meaning he has been through the mill – twice. He was the third of seven children born to labourers in the remote village of Sekhukhune, Limpopo. As his parents were working far away in Johannesburg, he had to fend for himself for months on end.

'So now the problem was what to do in those two months when they were not around. You struggle to get money to buy bread, to even eat during break time at school, and to pay for school trips. If your parents are not around, it becomes difficult. The money that they gave to me, I would rather maximise and multiply it, so that I don't have to ask them for more. If they gave me R10 or R20, I would buy a box of apples, sell them, make R30 and buy some more. I always had a profit of about 50 per cent or more, and I didn't have to ask anybody [for money] any more.'

Tebeila cracked a deal with local bus drivers to buy and deliver cheaper and fresher apples from the markets further away. It gave him a competitive edge when selling on the streets to discerning buyers without much money.

It was still a hard life. Every day, he walked barefoot through the mountains to school, 15 kilometres each way.

'It was very tough. In winter, you had to wake up at 4 o'clock, and every day you were still late. I was lashed for being late every day for two years,' Tebeila recalls.

To make a hard life even harder, he was drawn into politics, and became a leader in the South African Youth Congress (SAYCO), regarded as the most significant youth organisation to emerge during the 1980s. SAYCO's goals were to unite and politicise the youth in order to bring about the end of the state of emergency, and to agitate for the release of Nelson Mandela and the unbanning of the ANC and other organisations.

When the authorities cracked down on members of SAYCO, the

mountains of Limpopo, once Tebeila's obstacle on the way to school, became his friend. He would often stay in the mountains overnight to avoid arrest, suffering the freezing conditions without complaint.

When the apartheid regime started crumbling, the young, nimble Tebeila decided that the only way out for him was to make his own money.

'I would earn R20 and take it to my mother. Children usually want to buy things for themselves, but I bought curtains for the house at a jumble sale. I liked shopping at jumble sales, because I saw that I could buy so much more there than at a regular shop.'

Even then, Tebeila desperately wanted more. He believed he was an entrepreneur and was eager for a chance to prove it to the world.

'I think entrepreneurs are born – they are not made. It is a talent, like being a soccer player, but you have to nurture that talent,' he says. 'The environment dictates to you what you should do to meet the needs of the situation. You can't fold your arms if you are in a poverty-stricken environment, as that's where you start moving up. I have been selling all my life.'

When Tebeila finished school, he became a teacher. Along with nursing and the civil service, teaching was seen as a respectable profession, one of only a few recourses for aspiring black South Africans, as they were barred from many other jobs.

Tebeila got his first teaching job in Tembisa, east of Johannesburg, in 1989, but continued as an activist, recruiting members for banned organisations in the schools. It eventually cost him his job. The Department of Education fired him without even telling him. To make matters worse, the authorities banned him in both Gauteng and his home province of Limpopo, which meant that his movements were restricted and he could not associate with more than one person at a time. It made work and everyday life almost impossible.

Tebeila was unemployed for four months and was basically bankrupt; he even went into arrears on the bed he had bought with his first pay cheque. During this time, he survived on half a loaf of bread a day and a five-litre bottle of Oros, which he would eke out for two weeks.

Fortunately for him, there was a shortage of teachers in KwaNdebele in Mpumalanga, but the job came with a very low salary. So Tebeila started selling insurance on the side to his colleagues. Within a few months, he was earning 12 times the money he got for teaching.

He was emboldened enough to go for an interview with Sanlam, one of the giants of the South African insurance industry.

'When my friend took me for the interview at Sanlam, the manager couldn't understand me. He said, "Why are you here?" And I said, "I am here for an interview. I want to join full-time as an agent." He said to me, "You are a joke," because of the way I was dressed. It wasn't appealing to anybody. I was wearing traditional clothes from home. It was not nice, because you expect a person to come to an interview wearing a suit and tie, because of the job we would do and having to meet with clients. The manager said, "Sorry, we won't even consider you."

'Now my friend who was with me knew my strength and said, "If you don't take him, I'm leaving, because this is the man who is making me so much money. He has been working with me as a part-time agent." The manager then decided to take me. In my first year, in 1992, my salary was R17 000 in February, and I was not happy. But it was already more money than the annual salary of a teacher. I won so many awards at Sanlam from the first year. I was the top agent, Man of the Year, and was given many other awards.'

With the advent of democracy in 1994, the life-insurance industry started to open up. For a start, the new government appointed many more black people in better-paid public-service jobs. It created a whole new market for insurance, and in 1995 Tebeila opened his own broker-age, Morethi Insurance Brokers, with the commission he had made. He had a laptop, a desk and a small office.

'I wanted the freedom to sell other insurance products,' he says, 'and I also wanted to be independent. I had done really well, and I didn't see the need to report to anyone else any more.'

But he found going it alone stressful; cash flow was a problem. Tebeila refused to borrow money to keep the business afloat. He soon ran into arrears to the point where the sheriff of the court threatened to attach his property to settle his debts. Once again, he suffered, saved, went hungry and eventually rescued his business.

His next venture was to take advantage of the huge infrastructure gap the government faced. For a start, there were too many people and too few houses. Tebeila launched Tebcon, which soon became the largest black-owned construction company in Limpopo, the same province where he was once banned.

Then it was mining, which was to deliver Tebeila's hardest, and also most unexpected, business blow.

'My dream was always to own a mine and to build a conglomerate similar to that of Anglo American. My belief was very simple: when the Oppenheimer family started Anglo American, they started the same way I did. Not by buying other companies, but getting their own rights and developing them.'

But obtaining these mining rights proved more of a nightmare than a dream. Tebeila was turned down 10 times; each time he would collapse on the couch in his Polokwane office and fall asleep out of sheer frustration. In 2002, he used his last R100 000 to pay consultants in pursuit of yet another mining right. He found out too late that the money was non-refundable and ended up losing both the rights and the cash.

Then, in 2004, he identified the coal mine that he felt could make his fortune. He prayed for better luck. Soutpansberg contained an estimated 200 million tons of metallurgical coal and was spread across 11 farms, covering 8 000 hectares. It is situated near Messina, on the border with Zimbabwe, in Tebeila's home turf of Limpopo Province. On 19 April 2005, the government granted Tebeila a licence for the site, and he was ready to do business.

The only problem was that he did not have any money left to look for coal, and the banks wouldn't lend him any. He needed R1.5 million for exploration, and struck on the idea – as was fashionable in the first years of BEE – of gathering the money from the villagers who lived close to where he had grown up; people who had known him since birth.

So, on a crisp winter's morning near Bela-Bela, in the heart of the country's rich, massive northern Waterberg coalfields, hundreds of curious villagers gathered to hear what their brother, from whom many had bought apples years before, planned to do with his mining rights in return for their life savings.

'I remember it was a very cold day and I had a stomach problem ... There were many people there that day: old people, disabled people and even chiefs from the community. I told them that I needed their money and could make them all rich,' Tebeila says. He made a bold pitch, and all he could do that night was sleep, not too soundly, and wait.

The next day, a blind woman shuffled into Tebeila's office, holding onto the arm of one of her children, and handed over R15 000 in cash – her life savings.

'It is all I have. Spend it well, my son,' the woman said. Tebeila was humbled.

'It touched me a lot, and it showed belief in the project. The chiefs followed, and they represented the community. My feeling was that at least we have got people who are backing my dreams and who believe in my dreams. After all the stress of turned-down applications, this was going to be it.'

Flushed with cash and full of hope, Tebeila paid a firm of geological consultants R600 000 and drillers R900 000 to explore for coal at Soutpansberg.

Little did he know that his worst luck yet was about to strike.

Tebeila started hearing the alarm bells ringing when he spent weeks chasing up the consultants, without success. He decided to pay them a visit and, to his horror, found that the firm – which had been riven by strife – had dissolved overnight. To make matters worse, the geologist had fled to Australia with the exploration report under his arm. It meant Tebeila was mired in a project without information, money or hope. It was a test of character like no other in his decades in the business world. It could have been the end of him, and for the people who had shown such faith in him when they handed him their life savings.

'These people didn't even have a vision to be in the mining business, but I pulled them into it,' Tebeila recalls. 'And now I had lost all their money. My gut feeling was not to tell them what had happened, because it was going to be catastrophic. I had to find a solution, because I was the visionary.

'I never told anybody. I couldn't tell them we had lost their money. *I* could afford to be disappointed, but not other people. I couldn't phone a blind person, who had given me her last money, to tell her that I had lost everything...

'I was down and felt very bad. This was my second loss. I got that money through struggling and now it was gone. I was very down, but I never thought of quitting. Every time I had hardship, I always went and slept in my office. I went back and slept on my couch. I slept for four hours. I do this because it is both meditation and praying for an answer. I woke up with the solution.'

The answer lay in a laboratory in nearby Witbank. Because Tebeila had been hands-on during the exploration phase, he knew which laboratory the runaway consultant had used. He sped to the town, more in desperation than with any expectations.

There, Lady Luck at last smiled on Tebeila and the Soutpansberg coal project. The laboratory was able to salvage two pages of exploration data, which Tebeila clasped to his chest in relief. Luckily, they contained the all-important drilling data. It was a lifeline for the coal mine and, for Tebeila, manna from heaven. From those two pages, an expert could reconstruct the entire report on the coal project.

But it was mere respite; the struggle was far from over. With the two pages in hand, Tebeila spent five months trying to sell the idea of a coal mine to potential investors. There was a glimmer of hope when Brazilian resources giant Vale – the driving force behind Mozambique's mighty Moatize coal project – showed interest, but there was a language hurdle. Vale had to send the mining proposals to Brazil for translation into Portuguese, but this would take months, and Tebeila had neither the time nor the money.

At last, the sun finally broke through the clouds for the Soutpansberg project and its 200 million tons of metallurgical coal. While he was driving in his car, Tebeila received a phone call from Coal of Africa, a solid, established player in the South African mining industry.

As Tebeila recalls: 'Coal of Africa offered to purchase 74 per cent of the assets for R70 million. They also pledged to spend R100 million to take the project to a bankable feasibility study. It's the biggest deal I have ever closed on a cellphone while I was driving. The following day, they signed. Two years later, they offered me R20 million for the remaining 26 per cent. And gave me the capital to finance my present project, Waterberg Colliery, which will mine up to 15 million tons of coal a year by 2019.'

Sekoko Resources, the company that Tebeila founded in 2004, survived, diversified into iron ore, and is set to reach a turnover of R10 billion a year by 2019. And the people who gave Tebeila their last bundles of cash back in 2005?

'They got their dividends,' he smiles. 'They got all their money back, and they made a 300 per cent profit. Some built houses with that money. I felt very proud.'

So, as they say, coal's well that ends well ...

Tebeila says, 'I think I have learnt the art of perseverance. I learnt to persevere no matter what I do. I learnt to stick to my dreams. I want to build a new Anglo American, and I am doing that.'

His new venture is to build smartphones, which are usually imported from China by the ton, in Johannesburg. In May 2016, Sekoko Smartphones began building the devices at its Robertsham factory and is now producing 700 units a day. There is a booming cellphone market in Africa, and Sekoko aims to become a major player. Establishing the company cost a million dollars, and it currently employs 150 people. It is a bold venture in difficult economic times for South Africa, and it didn't get off to a great start either. Fallouts among the partners stalled the venture at one point, but it is now slowly but surely making inroads into the continent.

'We have established a network service provider called ETN,' Tebeila explains. 'So now we will sell cellphones to the network. Instead of running around searching for a market, I create my own market under the ETN network. The network is now in Sierra Leone and the Democratic Republic of Congo. We are buying into other companies in South Sudan.

We will be expanding, and I'm working day and night to increase our footprint in Africa. In three years, we should be in five countries. We will be a mobile network with its own phones on all ranges and tablets. Anybody who uses our network can also use our Sekoko phones.'

It may be an odd venture for Tebeila, the coal and construction man, but you have to give him credit for surviving some very tough times and emerging strong and resilient to become a multimillionaire.

Tebeila is driving back from the phone factory and thinking about his next entrepreneurial opportunity. He turns to *Forbes Africa* in the back seat and shares his idea, which is to build a bakery.

'I like bread,' he says wistfully.

Tebeila has managed to overcome great adversity on his journey to riches – surely baking bread will be easy enough? But one never knows with Tim Tebeila ...

7

The sage elder of Africa who studied with Mick Jagger

Pascal Dozie

Pascal Dozie

H E IS THE grand old man of African business: tall, imposing, a gentleman with impeccable manners. One of the big cheeses of Nigeria, he built a bank and catapulted his country into the cellphone era.

Pascal Dozie is one of the sages of West African business. Deeply concerned about the challenges his country faces, he also has strong, salty ideas on how to overcome them.

Dozie made his fortune by backing a couple of bright ideas with strong conviction, but now he fears for the younger generation. In 2016, the oil price dropped through the floor and the Nigerian currency, the naira, struggled. Then the government placed restrictions on the US dollar, which for so long has been a crutch for Nigeria's often chaotic, flagging economy.

'The whole macroeconomic scene is a little harsh,' Dozie says, 'but I believe it's a cycle. It will improve as Nigeria makes use of the opportunity that has been thrust on us by the world economy and [falling] oil prices. If we succeed in diversifying Nigeria's economy, then I think we will be in a more stable condition.'

Visiting Dozie on a hot afternoon in Lagos, I am witness to the very problems he is so passionate about solving. It is a nightmare drive across the crowded city. Horns hoot angrily as battered old cars veer within inches of each other on roads choked with traffic. Every now and again, a splash of dirty water from a pothole as a car ploughs through it sends a ripple of anger through the pedestrians walking on the side of the road.

To add injury to chaos, a pink-shirted traffic official is slowing down the arthritic progress even more by pulling drivers over for no apparent reason. When it is our turn, our driver takes exception and he and the traffic cop get into a finger-jabbing argument. I have spent more than 30 years in newsrooms and heard language that would make even the devil blush, but this was something else. On this day, sitting in the passenger seat with fingers jabbing inches from my nose, I feel like a monk in Gomorrah.

'They just want money,' scowls the driver as we eventually crawl away from the scene in bumper-to-bumper traffic that stretches far over the horizon – well, as far as you can see through the pollution. The driver sounds resigned.

As we near Dozie's plush, air-conditioned office, we happen upon a pothole filled with water, wide and deep enough in which to breed fish. Nigeria's challenges lead right up to the door of the multimillionaire who so dearly wants to fix them, I think to myself.

'Lagos is the only place in the world where you can utilise all the faculties God gave to man,' Dozie chuckles when I later recount my experience on the road.

From this office in Lagos, Dozie oversees his business empire. He is one of the wealthiest and most respected men in Nigeria, but he is soft-spoken, almost paternal – a gentleman who chooses his words carefully. But he speaks with warmth and a sprinkle of humour when he talks about the absurdities of life.

The refined, polished surfaces of his office contrast vividly with the dog-eat-dog desperation out on the streets. Dozie could be forgiven if he decided to shut the tall gates on the rest of Nigeria after half a century of business, but that's not who he is.

'We won't get anywhere until we, in Nigeria, can say anything can be done in 24 hours,' he says. 'Many people see Nigeria as an entrepreneur's gold mine – opportunities abound. Every single disadvantage you see – the traffic and the infrastructure – is an opportunity, but you can only effect change once the government is hands-off.'

How likely is that? I counter. A few years back I attended a conference in Kigali, where Uganda's President Yoweri Museveni said that it was easier for a camel to pass through the eye of a needle than it was to keep government out of business.

'We have been moving towards this for a long time in Nigeria,' Dozie claims. 'If the government was not hands-off, we would not have a number of major cellphones in the country; some of them got their operating licences on the same day. This hands-off approach has helped us leapfrog communications technology.'

Like the driver who drove me to his office, Dozie's biggest concern is corruption.

'This is the only country in the world where people ask what business are you in and you say, "Politics".'

Dozie believes that the people of Africa, and especially the youth, have had enough. According to him, social media is allowing for more transparency, making it more difficult to cover up corruption.

'Nigerians are waking up, and the civil society in this country is coming alive. Nigeria is a country that is skewed towards the youth. Young people are using Twitter and Facebook, and you should see the things they are writing.'

Twitter and Facebook are about as far away as you can get from Dozie's country roots. He was born on 9 April 1939, the son of a court interpreter, in Owerri, Imo State, in eastern Nigeria, seven hours' drive from Lagos.

'We did not have many modern facilities, but we had the village set-up. If you were hungry, someone would feed you. If your neighbour caught you doing something wrong, they would punish you. When your parents found out, they would talk to the neighbour to make sure they had given you a proper spanking. Modernity has changed all of that.'

To say Dozie is close to his Igbo roots is like saying a tortoise is close to its shell. He made sure that his culture was passed on to his children.

'We didn't see my father that often when we were growing up,' says Uzoma Dozie, one of Dozie's sons, 'but when he came home to see us, it was really quality time. We would sit outside for hours while he told us stories and sang the songs of his ancestors. It was beautiful.'

In the early 1960s, newly independent Nigeria was changing apace. In these heady and idealistic early years of independence, many African nations sent their youngest and brightest to study in the former colonial capitals. Dozie was one of them. He went to study at the London School of Economics (LSE), where one of his fellow students was a long-haired wannabe who was obsessed with Muddy Waters, Howlin' Wolf, Robert Johnson and the blues – Mick Jagger.

'I knew him,' says Dozie with a broad smile, about as near to starstruck as he will ever be.

The manner of Jagger's exit from the LSE in 1963 is still a matter of conjecture. A politician I knew years ago told me that the Rolling Stones frontman had stood up in a lecture one day and cried: 'Eureka!' before walking out to a life of stardom. The reality is not as dramatic and clear-cut. Jagger studied economics and earned average grades. But he kept on studying, just in case the Rolling Stones proved to be a flash in the pan. When the group cut its first single, in June 1963, he left the LSE.

'We thought [Mick] was different,' recalls Dozie. 'We were very conservative and he had long hair. As an African, coming from Nigeria, I couldn't believe that he was giving up his studies to go and play music. It went against the grain for me. In the village where I grew up, you only played music if you had nothing else to do.'

Unlike Jagger, Dozie completed his degree in economics and then obtained a master's degree in administration from City University in London. He laid the foundations of his career with his first job, at the National Economic Development Office (NEDO) in Croydon, south London. He was one of many expatriate Africans to work there. NEDO was established to support the National Economic Development Council (NEDC), which was a corporatist economic planning forum set up in 1962 in the United Kingdom to bring together management, trade unions and government in an attempt to address Britain's relative economic decline.

Although Dozie dearly wanted to go home during his time in London, the war that was tearing his country apart prevented him from doing so. Back home, his two brothers were fighting for the Igbo people in Biafra's secession from Nigeria. The Biafran War was bloody and brutal and lasted from 1967 to 1970. Overall, there were 100 000 military casualties, while between 500 000 and two million Biafran civilians died from starvation. Dozie watched in horror from London as the war unfolded.

'It was a very traumatic period for us. Bombs were going off everywhere and you didn't know what the truth was. People were being shunted from one place to another, and at times I didn't even know where my own mother was.' The pain is still etched on his face nearly half a century on.

Dozie decided to take a job in Uganda, knowing that he was going to be in exile until peace was brokered in his homeland. He finally moved back home in September 1971 to look after his mother, who by then was in poor health.

Back in Lagos, the first thing Dozie did was to set up his own consultancy, which he called the African Development Consulting Group (ADCG). He would never work for anyone else again.

In the early days of the business, ADCG was fortunate enough to be awarded plum consultancy contracts from big players like Nestlé and Pfizer. In his spare time, Dozie wrote articles on economics for heavyweight publication *Business International*.

Then, in the 1980s, the road to real riches opened up for Dozie, thanks to a simple idea that had occurred on a dusty and often dangerous road that stretched across his country.

For years, Dozie had observed the problems of the traders who had to travel to Lagos from the villages of eastern Nigeria, where he grew up. Many of the traders had to carry huge bundles of cash if they wanted to do business in the big city, and sometimes they would be waylaid by thieves and robbers.

Dozie's inspired idea was to implement a system whereby the traders could make electronic bank transfers so that they would not have to risk carrying any cash. As a result of his brainwave, the Diamond Bank was established in 1991.

'The first customer was my wife,' Dozie laughs.

Today, Diamond Bank may be one of the biggest names in Nigerian banking, but it had a humble beginning, in a tiny third-floor office in Victoria Island with 20 people and $5 million in cash.

'The assumption was that we were going to come by money easily – it wasn't easy,' Dozie remembers.

In those conservative days, most businesses didn't want to deal with a bank less than three years old, as new banks were seen as fly-by-night operations. So the tiny staff at Diamond Bank hit the streets to persuade everyone, from traders to car dealers, to make deposits so that the bank could generate cash. The strategy paid off, and Dozie's resilience and ingenuity won him many admirers in the banking industry.

Said Akinbamidele Akintola, then of Renaissance Capital in Lagos, 'In my view, Dozie is brilliant. [He is] driven and a great manager of talent – qualities which helped him in establishing Diamond Bank, especially through the five-year period from 1985 to 1990, when nothing was happening, and the early years from 1990, when he says they really had it tough.'

With Dozie and his staff's hard work and dedication, the bank blossomed into a $240-million concern. But it proved merely the first step on a difficult path. In 2005, the bank took a knock when the government passed a new law decreeing that all banks had to retain a minimum of 25 billion naira (around $158 million) in share capital. Diamond Bank had only 6.4 billion naira (around $40 million), and it was forced to list to raise more. This diluted the family's stake, but at least the bank survived.

But the deal that would make Dozie's name was far more daring – a 1998 venture with South African cellphone company MTN, which was staking its claim throughout Africa. MTN management approached Dozie with the idea of setting up a network in the potentially vast Nigerian market. The South Africans would invest millions of rands in a 60 per cent stake in MTN Nigeria, with Nigerians owning the rest.

With high hopes, Dozie set off for London and the United States to sell the idea to wealthy Nigerian expatriates and the big money men, but he was soon discouraged by their lack of enthusiasm. It was as if he was trying to sell sand in the desert.

Potential investors pointed out that Nigeria's state telecoms company,

NITEL, with its sparse and unreliable landlines, was struggling. If the state couldn't set up a cellphone network in Nigeria, no one could, they told Dozie.

'It was very disappointing,' Dozie says. 'You have a good project and you are turned down. You start to question yourself and start to question your [own decision-making].'

Dozie could raise only 20 per cent of the capital needed for the new company. But MTN was not about to give up. They obtained the millions needed to get the project off the ground through debt-funding and, although it was a huge risk at the time, MTN prospered and had nearly 60 million subscribers in Nigeria in 2016.

Says Dozie: 'Most of the people I asked to invest now regret not investing – I even regret it myself. They would have enjoyed returns of 20 times their money.'

More than a decade older and wiser today, Dozie runs a family investment company, Kunoch, valued at $50 million, which is involved in industries ranging from power generation to gas processing, oil exploration, real estate and banking. If you have a plan and a feasibility study, Dozie is the man who will hear you out. The company focuses primarily on power projects, particularly on building infrastructure. The Murtala Muhammed International Airport in Lagos, which is the international gateway to Nigeria, is a focus point for the company. Many foreign business people have stood cursing and sweating in the long queues at that airport, vowing never to return to Nigeria if they ever escaped from it. Dozie is only too aware of this.

'It erodes the image of the country. When you come through our airport, you say, "Is this the Nigeria I have come to see?"'

In 2012, Dozie believed that the government would privatise the airport in a bid to improve it, despite opposition from certain unions and government fears of losing control.

'I will give it a long shot; it will happen in the next five years.'

It wasn't too long a shot. In August 2016, newspapers in Nigeria reported that the Federal Airports Authority of Nigeria was seriously considering privatising the airports in Lagos and Abuja.

What about the bugbear of corruption?

'It is very solvable. When we start seeing politics as a sacrifice, when it is a self-sacrificing exercise from those who want to serve ... We need strong institutions with integrity and political parties with a well-known ideology.'

When I ask Dozie what role the entrepreneurs of Africa can play in advancing the continent and its people, he becomes more animated.

'I think [entrepreneurs] are counting on the political will of African leaders to smooth logistics, the factors of production and the movement of people. There are a lot of bottlenecks that need to be removed. People like Aliko Dangote have served us well and created a lot of employment. For me, what is lacking here is that we don't have the critical mass in the genuine middle class, which is the bulwark of democracy. Once this happens, we could start absorbing young people into employment and our creative forces will be unleashed,' he explains. 'We all worry about food, shelter and health, and, until those things are made accessible to all people, [conditions] will never change ... Be patient; don't expect miracles to happen.'

As 2016 drew to a close, Dozie, who is in his late 70s, was semi-retired but still keeping a finger in a few pies. These included teaming up with the government to look for gold, and investing in hotels and the railroad. The latter has been one of the abandoned, rusting car wrecks of the Nigerian economy, resuscitated in the last decade with the help of Chinese money.

'We just found a young man who is enthusiastic about the economic potential of efficient railroads, and we are encouraging him. He is championing the rail spirit and he is going to change the way goods move in Nigeria,' Dozie says in the twilight years of his life as an entrepreneur. 'I have no regrets. There are certain things one could have done. At my age, you find that there are certain decisions you can take in a very clinical way and considering nothing but the business case. But also, when it touches on the human element, you turn softer, and by the time you look at it, you are more or less a coach trying to give advice. It takes time, and sometimes you are not looking at the quick ways, you are looking at the longer term and how to make an impact; that's what matters.'

In his yearning for a new Nigeria, Dozie draws inspiration from one of the entrepreneurs he most admires, the late Steve Jobs.

'I loved his never-quit spirit. He lost his position in the company, but he did not despair,' says Dozie.

Jobs built a world-class brand. Had he been handed the task of building a new Nigeria, he may very well have been tempted to despair.

8

The Three Wise Men:
Brey, Robertson
and Brozin

Brey, Robertson and Brozin

Brey, Robertson
and Brozin

THEY ARE THREE of the unlikeliest partners in Africa and had the humblest of beginnings in business. A teacher and two accountants, they set out with a well-meaning idea that began in rather amateur fashion. To get their business up and running, they approached regular people who wrote them small cheques on their doorstep or in petrol stations on the boot of their car. They are three men from very different worlds – and three different religions. However, they shared one fear with the regular people who invested their money with them: financial losses.

Nelson Mandela was one of the first shareholders in this company, which would survive market crashes and world economic turmoil on its way to becoming hugely successful. Brimstone Investment survived it all, bloodied but unbowed. In the end, it is a lesson in how a combination of long-term investment, grassroots funding, street savvy and high finance can bring power to the people. These days, you could call it crowd-funding; 20 years ago, it was just business on a shoestring.

Mustaq Brey, Fred Robertson and Lawrie Brozin are the three musketeers who collected small-time investors' meagre offerings and turned them into gold. They have stuck together through thick and thin, sharing the same principles – number one being that the company would never invest in either gambling or alcohol.

On the face of it, they make an incongruous trio. Fred Robertson grew up in poverty in apartheid Cape Town; Mustaq Brey is a quiet accountant; Lawrie Brozin is a well-heeled, suit-wearing accountant from Johannesburg. They met by chance. Brozin's contribution was a large slice of seed capital from his wealthy Johannesburg family. Brey and Brozin are the backroom boys in the operation. It is the avuncular Robertson, with his ready smile and wit, who is the public face of Brimstone Investment.

Robertson grew up rough in District Six in Cape Town in the apartheid years. This colourful neighbourhood was home to the so-called coloured population of the city, but it was situated far too close for comfort to the white areas, and the authorities bulldozed it into oblivion in the 1970s. Their neighbourhood's destruction scattered the Robertson family, along with 60 000 of their neighbours, across the townships on the hungry, rundown margins of Cape Town, out of sight, out of mind.

'We were thrown across this piece of wasteland called the Cape Flats,' Robertson recalls. 'Families were torn apart. Friends and neighbours were separated. We were a family of nine children. My sisters were in different townships; our family disintegrated.'

The young Robertson grew up hustling a living on the streets of Cape Town, the city that didn't want him, selling newspapers and apples in a cinema. I interviewed him years later, when he was a candidate and I a judge for CNBC Africa's All Africa Business Leaders Awards (AABLA), and I gained some insight into the straightforward, uncomplicated man he has become.

One of the questions the judges had to ask all the candidates was whether they come from family money. In other words, did the entrepreneurs make their own fortune, or were they backed by the family coffers?

'Did you have any family money, Fred?' I asked.

'Yes,' he replied, to my surprise. 'My father used to give me a few shillings a week when I was a kid.'

I laughed and told him that pocket money didn't count, but his frank answer was one of the reasons why he won the 2015 AABLA Entrepreneur of the Year Award.

Yes, indeed, Robertson has made his money the hard way. He started on the road to fortune by becoming a teacher. For many coloured men of the time, this was the highest position in society they could aspire to. But Robertson eventually quit this safe job, as he wanted to be in business. He decided to learn about investing and joined South African life assurance giant Old Mutual, selling insurance door to door. It was no easy row to hoe; his patch included the remote, small towns of the Northern Cape – a day's drive from Cape Town.

'I used to have to sleep in the car park at a petrol station overnight and ask the guys working the petrol pumps to let me use the toilets so I could freshen up before I went to see my customers in the morning,' he reflects. More than 20 years later, he sits on the board of Old Mutual.

His rise from foot soldier to boardroom boss was prompted by an epiphany he and Brey had in the United States in 1994, when South Africa was in the first flush of democracy. The two had been friends for years and shared an interest in politics. As emergent black businessmen, they had travelled to the US with the Department of Foreign Affairs to campaign for American investment in South Africa, and came back with the idea that would make them their fortune.

'The idea was born out of the freedom of our country,' Robertson says. 'We had achieved political liberation, but we knew there was going to be economic liberation as well. Because before that, as black people, we couldn't do business in the main streets of South Africa. That's what inspired us.'

Brey and Robertson returned to Cape Town for what they called a hard year's slog. They rented a 9 x 3 metre office for R500 (around $150) a month and started to raise money for Brimstone, their new company.

The third member of their team joined Brimstone in 1995, an association that began with a chance conversation over a whiskey between Robertson and the Brozin family in their home in the plush Illovo suburb of Johannesburg. The Brozins are well-known entrepreneurs in South Africa; Robbie Brozin, Lawrie's brother, was one of the founders of Nando's, the world-famous peri-peri chicken franchise.

Says Lawrie Brozin 20 years later: 'Fred was telling me about Brimstone. I said it sounded interesting. Fred said I should come down to Cape Town and meet his partner, who was Mustaq. We were both colleagues, both accountants, very similar backgrounds, but from very diverse communities. And I said I am happy to throw in my lot with him.'

Lawrie's father Max, who was in the electronics business, pumped R1.5 million (about $400 000) into the business as an interest-free loan.

'Thankfully, we've already paid him back,' chuckles Brozin two decades later.

When Robertson, Brozin and Brey joined forces, their first big deal was already underway. The only problem was that they didn't have enough money to finance it. They called it the Oceana deal, and it would be the first milestone in Brimstone's investment journey: a 9.73 per cent stake in the Oceana Group, a collection of operating subsidiaries in the fishing and cold-storage industries along South Africa's West Coast.

Recalls Brey: 'The bank told us they would lend us R4 million ($1.1 million). We had to raise another R3 million ($842 000) ourselves in six weeks. We went door to door. I even remember organising a bond on one shareholder's house to get some money.'

One of the first investors they signed up was a man in a grease-covered overall amid the noise and petrol fumes of the Aden Service Station in Athlone on the Cape Flats. He was 37-year-old Makkie Isaacs. Like Robertson, he too had been bulldozed out of District Six. Makkie's father was a vegetable hawker who had saved every penny to buy the patch of land on which the family then built the Aden Service Station.

On this day, in 1995, Robertson and Brey were among the many filling up their cars on the forecourt of Isaacs's petrol station.

'As they were filling up, they said to me: "Makkie, we're starting this company. Do you want to invest in it?" They were like two men collecting for a charity or a mosque. I said to them that they didn't need to explain anything to me,' says Isaacs. He wiped his hands, took out his pen from his top pocket and wrote a cheque for R15 000 (about $4 000) on the boot of a brown Audi.

A few days later, Robertson and Brey contacted Isaacs and told him that they needed only R12 000. They asked him what they should do with the surplus amount.

'I innocently told them to use it for petrol or anything else they needed it for,' says Isaacs. 'I think I was share certificate number seven. I never expected a return from them. When Fred has his AGMs, he mentions how he went door to door to get people to invest in his company. It was just a start-up company, where people believed in the management, not the business. People believed in Mustaq Brey and Fred Robertson.'

More than two decades later, that cheque, written more in faith than with conviction, has multiplied 34 times, helping to make Isaacs a very wealthy man.

The small amounts of cash that the mechanics, fishermen, teachers and blue-collar workers of Cape Town put into Oceana would result in Brimstone's first successful deal. It got people talking and even caught the eye of the country's president, Nelson Mandela.

'Mandela was one of our first shareholders,' Robertson remembers with a chuckle. 'He paid for his shares, just like everybody else. He read about us in the newspaper and called us to the Presidency and said he would also like to invest. And we said, "Yes, of course."'

'He bought 240 000 shares with a cheque of R300 000 (around $80 000),' adds Brey.

It had been a fair-weather start for Brimstone, and its sails billowed into favourable trade winds; but foul weather loomed on the horizon.

The years 1995 and 1996 saw a huge boom in the stock market in South Africa. Investors were optimistic about the new Rainbow Nation, and the liberalisation of the economy benefitted business all round. The Johannesburg Stock Exchange reformed and modernised rapidly to open up a huge flow of investment into the markets.

'Everyone was listing,' says Brozin. 'We used my house as an office in Illovo. We had cigars and whisky. It was such a crazy time. We became quite substantial after a year, because the market carried us. Then the music stopped.'

The financial storm started gathering in August 1997, when share prices started falling, and the market woes continued into 1998, when Brimstone listed on the JSE. It happened with the usual fanfare and a live TV link between the shareholders of Cape Town and the trading floor in Johannesburg. But it would prove a horror show for Brimstone.

'The world financial markets were in turmoil,' Brey recalls. 'At the time we listed, [our share price] had gone up to R6 ($1.68). Our INAV [indicative net asset value – the measure of the net asset value of an investment based on assets less liabilities] was then R2.50 ($0.35).'

By the end of 1998, the Brimstone share price, along with Mandela's money, was heading for rock bottom.

'Then the vultures starting circling and said they wanted to buy us out,' Brey recalls. 'They told us we could make R150 million (about $30 million). A financial group in Johannesburg approached us and suggested that we delist Brimstone, buy the shareholders out at the current market price, buy them out for a rand, sell all the assets and make R1.50 (30 US cents) profit on every share.

'But we said we don't want to leave Cape Town. We took money from the people of the Cape Flats; we'd have to flee Cape Town if word got out that we'd done something like that. It was unethical. What we then decided to do was sell off all liquid or listed stocks, the easily sellable stuff. Turn that R1.50 and give back capital of R1.50 to our shareholders. Our shareholders liked it, but the market didn't. Our price went down to 20 cents ($0.03) in October 2001.'

Adds Brozin, shaking his head, 'At the lowest of the low, our share [traded at] 18 cents.'

In those days, you couldn't even buy chewing gum for that.

But somehow Brimstone weathered the storm, and looked towards the ocean for its salvation. In 2003, the company doubled its stake in Sea Harvest, one of the largest hake producers along South Africa's West Coast, to 61.44 per cent; Sea Harvest processes 40 000 tons of fish in Saldanha, as well as at Mossel Bay on the Indian Ocean.

A dozen years later, the gross value of this stake is worth $52 million. As confidence in their business grew, Brimstone acquired shares in some of the biggest businesses in South Africa: Old Mutual, for whom Robertson used to sell insurance, worth $22.4 million; Nedbank, worth $47.5 million, and Life Healthcare, worth $202 million. The Oceana deal, which had helped Brimstone set sail, is now worth a hefty $162 million.

There was a bit of calm for Brimstone before the next financial storm occurred. This time it was the global financial crisis of 2008, with big names like Lehman Brothers of New York running aground when the United States property bubble burst, causing worldwide panic.

Although it should have had little to do with Brimstone and South Africa, with its rigid exchange controls, the whole world, from Cape Town to New York, was affected. Even today, some investors and other experts believe that the hangover from those desperate days is far from over.

The financial crisis hit Brimstone hard. Its headline earnings dropped from $69.9 million in 2007 to a loss of $7.1 million. By the end of 2008, Brimstone had lost 7.7 per cent of its value, according to company figures. If ever Brimstone had taken a battering in a financial storm, this was it.

But there was some relief in the morning; to the rescue rode a lifesaver in more ways than one. The Life Healthcare deal, struck in 2005, matured in 2010, just in time to save the company. Brimstone unbundled the company and created wealth for its long-suffering shareholders. The move shook off the ravages of recession and stabilised the company, and it also meant that the trio could hold their heads up high in Cape Town.

Life Healthcare was a wise investment at a time when South Africa had a growing, ageing middle class, coupled with a cash-strapped public health system. Never before had people paid so much for health treatment. Brimstone has a 5.04 per cent stake in Life Healthcare. That alone is worth more than $200 million.

'Over the past 10 years, Brimstone has delivered an annual total return of over 40 per cent to its investors,' says Mia Kruger, director, equity analyst and portfolio manager at Kruger International, a private wealth investment company. 'Over the past year, Brimstone's exposure to the fishing industry, through Oceana Group and Sea Harvest, as well as its investment in Tiger Brands, has boosted its performance. The underlying assets allow investors the opportunity to get exposure to unlisted companies with good earnings growth.'

But it has rarely been plain sailing for Brimstone. I remember the fiery anger in Robertson's eyes one day in 2015, when he told me about

Brimstone's latest disaster. The company had placed people it thought it could trust at the insurance company Lion of Africa, which it owns, only to find out that a number of staff were encouraging family members to file fraudulent insurance claims, in effect stealing millions from the company.

'We thought we could trust them, and we were let down,' says Robertson.

Brimstone called in the police, which cost it a lot of pride and resulted in a R275-million loss.

But today, Brey is happy with the company: 'Our results were positively impacted by the turnaround of Lion of Africa. The remedial action and strategic changes at Lion have started to yield positive results. The turnaround was achieved by more stringent risk-acceptance procedures and the deployment of a new, experienced executive team. Lion of Africa is now firmly on the right track and is clawing its way back into the market, reclaiming its position as a truly South African insurer.'

Brimstone was famous for its results meetings, which used to be lavish affairs. Shareholders would party to loud music after the number-crunching was over. The small gathering in June 2016 at the Taj Cape Town was low-key by comparison. There was no music; only a few men in suits. And the books were looking a bit brighter than the winter weather outside. Just about two decades after the first cheque was signed at a petrol station on the boot of that brown Audi, Brimstone's assets totalled R7.3 billion, with an intrinsic net asset value of R4.2 billion.

In 2016, Brimstone went on an acquisition spree around the world. It again looked towards the sea for profits. In May, a R274-million share-purchase agreement between Brimstone Investment and Kagiso Strategic Investments III Proprietary Limited increased Brimstone's stake in Sea Harvest, which accounts for 15 per cent of its portfolio, to 85 per cent.

Robertson says: 'Our three largest investments – Oceana, Life Healthcare and Sea Harvest, which comprise over 65 per cent of our gross intrinsic asset value – all now have significant off-shore exposure through trading and investments in foreign geographies, including the US, India, Poland and Australia. The group will continue to maintain its positive long-term view on its investments and pursue value-accreting opportunities.'

Sea Harvest has itself been fishing, acquiring 59.6 per cent equity in Western Australia prawn kings Mareterram Trading in December 2015. Mareterram is listed on the Australian Stock Exchange and Sea Harvest has the largest shareholding in the company.

But the 2016 results presentation was also a sad time for Brimstone. The three musketeers were breaking up. Brozin had already retired by this winter presentation and new management was on the way in.

'The Fred and Mustaq show is about to end,' Brozin said with a hint of sadness at the Taj. It would be his last results presentation.

What the three of them will do in their retirement is anyone's guess. It is likely that Robertson – along with many of his 60 000 former neighbours – will try to reclaim his family's land in District Six. Nearly half a century since the bulldozers destroyed their home, the land still lies fallow. A few years ago, Robertson applied to the government to get the land back.

'We're waiting to hear from the government. Hopefully they won't give us our piece of land back. We're hoping they will get it wrong and give us one higher up on the hill instead. The views from there are much better!' he laughs. He is standing on Signal Hill, high above Cape Town, one windy day looking over the restless sea towards the slopes of his former home.

The desire to move up the hill, no matter what, and the choppy blue waters below are a fitting metaphor for Brimstone's patchy progress. The ocean is full of shipwrecks, proving that even the sturdiest vessels can flounder and sink in a violent storm. Brimstone was lucky not to join those wrecks during the worst financial storms in modern times.

9

From barefoot
to a $500-million
African media empire

Reginald Mengi

Reginald Mengi

'WHAT WOULD YOU say if I showed up barefoot and without a belt?' chuckles multimillionaire Reginald Mengi on the telephone as he discusses his photo shoot for the cover of *Forbes Africa*. It is a playful nod to his roots in the fields of northern Tanzania, as well as to his penchant for mischief and plain-speaking.

When he arrives at *Forbes Africa*'s offices in Sandton, he is dressed to the nines: designer shoes, a sharp Italian navy-blue pinstripe suit ... and a belt, of course. This speaks volumes of the man Mengi once was and the man he has become.

Mengi has capitalised on some spectacular pieces of luck en route to his super-wealthy status: he won a scholarship to Europe as a young boy, then years later saw a gap in the market and founded his first business, which set him on the road to spectacular wealth.

His is a remarkable story, from his humble beginnings to making his fortune in media and marrying a former Miss Tanzania. Nowadays he jets between Paris and Cape Town clad in Canali suits. He is dapper, with a firm handshake and a warm smile.

Mengi is the owner of a large, profitable media empire based in Tanzania's capital, Dar es Salaam. As one of Africa's most powerful media barons, he holds sway over the minds of millions of Africans. He is also a dyed-in-the-wool Africanist.

'For a long time we have been saying Africa is poor, but that's wrong. Africa, as a continent, is not poor; it's the people who are poor. We should open our eyes. Africa as a continent is very rich,' he says with conviction.

Mengi knows all about poverty. As a child he went barefoot and slept on a dirt floor in the town of Machame, near the slopes of Mount Kilimanjaro, in northern Tanzania. His parents owned a small plot where they toiled every day to feed their family of eight. Fortunately, Mengi's mother was a bit of an entrepreneur, and she taught the young Mengi a lot.

'My mother would take a bunch of bananas and come back with a kilo of rice. She would take just one chicken and come back with a kilo of potatoes; or a bunch of bananas and come back with a pair of shorts for school. That is the greatest entrepreneur I admire.'

Mrs Mengi may have been the mother of invention, but the family nevertheless always struggled.

'We lived in a mud hut with two cows, three sheep and a few chickens. Nothing more than that in terms of what my family was worth, because we just couldn't make ends meet … We couldn't afford food, and when we got two meals a day, it was a great celebration,' Mengi recalls.

But Mengi wanted more than two meals a day, and he took a long shot. He was in Form 5 in high school, with one year to go, when he applied for a scholarship to study accounting in Glasgow, Scotland. For a high-school child from Machame, it may as well have been the moon. Stranger still, the scholarship was granted.

'I couldn't tell my headmaster that I had won a scholarship to go to the UK halfway through Form 5, so I ran away from school.'

Friends and family tried to persuade Mengi to stay in Tanzania, but he had made up his mind. In 1970s Tanzania, overseas scholarships were rare; at the very least, they promised an air ticket. Mengi flew from Moshi to Nairobi and stopped off in London en route to Glasgow. The country boy had been told the streets of London were paved with gold, but he soon found out that they weren't.

'I saw a beggar on the street, a white beggar, and after that I said: "You know what? Even London has many things like home."'

When he arrived in Scotland, it was a lot warmer than he had dared imagine. As a child he had heard tales of draughty castles and the terrifying Loch Ness monster, but when he got to Scotland, it was the warmth of the people that impressed him most.

After a journey of more than 11 500 kilometres and ensconced at college in Glasgow, Mengi suddenly had a change of heart. He decided he no longer wanted to be an articled clerk at an accounting firm. He relayed his decision to his sponsors, who told him that he had to stay in Scotland and study for six months, whether he liked it or not.

Mengi didn't like it, and he abandoned the course. But he managed to stay in Scotland by taking on lowly jobs, and he enrolled in night school to complete his abandoned high-school studies. The work he found was a world away from the life of an articled clerk – he drove buses and worked long hours as a cleaner.

'I wouldn't turn [a job] down because it was too dirty or the money was too little. My reasoning was as follows: if I work, I get £1; if I don't do it, I get nothing ... One pound is better than nothing.'

Mengi's homespun philosophy on the value of money has guided him on his path to riches. Those tough early days also shaped the resilience and inventiveness that would aid him in his quest.

Mengi soon found his feet in the foreign land. Driving buses and cleaning floors helped the pounds to trickle in. But then, just as his financial situation was improving, tragic news arrived from Africa. His father had died, and Mengi did not have enough money to go home for the funeral. This is unthinkable for a son of Africa; to this day, Mengi reflects sadly on those painful days of mourning far from home.

'The biggest regret I had was that he passed away without me being able to show him that I'd been able to make something of my life, so that he could say: "Well, that's *my* son." That, I regret. I just wish he had lived for a while for me to go back and say, "Daddy, you know what, I've been able to make it, and please let me be by your side." That eats me up till today,' says Mengi, shaking his head gently in sorrow. He pulls a handkerchief from his well-tailored pocket to wipe away a tear.

With this pain at his core, Mengi was even more determined to make a go of life in Scotland. He finished his high-school studies and was offered a job by Cooper Brothers, now PricewaterhouseCoopers (PwC), where he completed his articles. He swiftly rose up the ranks of the company and became a member of the Institute of Chartered Accountants in England and Wales.

But although Mengi was cracking it in Scotland, he yearned for home. After nine years away, he transferred to the company's Nairobi office. When he got there, he realised he had made a mistake. He resigned a few hours after reporting for work – surely one of the shortest careers in the history of PwC. The call of his home, a short flight to the south, had proven too strong.

'I wanted to be in Tanzania. I knew I could make more money in Britain, but I wanted to go home. I wanted to go back and do something for my people. I was educated by poor Tanzanians, and I thought it would be good to give back.'

Armed with his overseas experience, Mengi spent a year in Moshi before securing a job with his old company, PwC, in Dar es Salaam. He worked hard, and at the age of 30 became one of the youngest partners in the company. At the height of his career at PwC, he was both chairman and managing partner. A life of lucrative comfort stretched before him. But then the contrary streak that had caused him to abandon his scholarship in Scotland returned – Mengi resigned.

'Some people leave their jobs when times are bad, but I left mine when things were really good. I couldn't wait around until things got bad and then leave. You must change when things are really good. You go into the new job with a big kind of energy, rather than going there totally depressed because you have been sucked dry or you were not doing that well.'

Mengi yearned to break into big business, but he was streetwise enough to know he had to start small. There were plenty of opportunities around in 1980s Tanzania. He recalls that he saw suffering and shortage everywhere in those days. The years of socialist economics had taken their toll on consumer goods and they were as rare as hen's teeth on the streets of the capital. The unintended consequence of this was that it yielded Mengi's first idea as an entrepreneur.

One day, Mengi ventured out onto the bustling streets of the capital to look for a pen. He couldn't believe it when he couldn't find one, and he'd spent the day searching high and low. Everyone needs a pen at some point, Mengi thought, as he spotted a gap in the market as wide as the Indian Ocean. He recruited a friend and they did their research. They found a pen-component manufacturer in Kenya and arranged to ship in the necessary items.

'When the components arrived, I didn't know where to put them, so the best place was my bedroom. It was in that bedroom that I started the assembly of the pens,' he recalls.

Scrabbling on his bedroom floor to put pens together was a huge step down from his big office at PwC, where Mengi had had staff and had enjoyed the luxury of a company house. These were hard times on the very bottom rung of business. Mengi worked a 16-hour day and made deliveries on foot. Overnight, the Peugeot 504 was downscaled to a 104. This dip in lifestyle was worth it, though, as in time the pen would prove mightier than PwC.

'That little business gave me my first million dollars,' Mengi remembers.

He was on a roll, selling his pens to the masses, and anything and everything at the high-volume, lower end of the market. There was shoe polish made from ground charcoal and oil, and a natural skin exfoliator that was simply bottled mud from the sea. There appeared to be no end to what Mengi could produce to make money: soap, toilet paper, detergent, beds, shoes, toothpaste.

'I made sure that no one in Tanzania could spend a day without coming into contact with or touching one of my products ... The only thing I couldn't produce at that time was the air that you breathe.'

Air was to come into it in the form of the airwaves, on which Mengi was about to spend his accumulated millions.

To paraphrase British newspaper magnate Lord Beaverbrook, you can print a million food labels a day, at a vast profit, and no one will even know your name; but if you print 10 000 copies of a newspaper, at a loss, everyone will invite you to lunch. It is all about influence.

Mengi had no experience in journalism, but he was clearly aware that the written and spoken word wielded great influence. And so he formed a media group, IPP Group, of which he took sole control. This was very important to Mengi as an entrepreneur.

In 1994, he bought *The Guardian* in Tanzania, and a year later, before he'd properly got his feet wet in the business, he launched Tanzania's first television network, ITV.

'We launched five years before government TV. There was a law in Tanzania that did not allow television. It was government censorship. My network was operating on the one hand as if it was national television, but on the other hand it was private television.'

Nearly a quarter of a century later, Mengi owns a string of newspapers, three radio stations and three television networks, with more than one thousand people working for him. He seems to have picked up the media business quickly, conceding that the only times he worries is when politicians praise him.

'If politicians start complimenting you, then you must be careful – there must be something wrong with what you are doing. To be criticised is healthy; it means you must be doing your job well in the media.'

Mengi says he believes in free speech, but concedes that there are limits in Africa.

'The images you see in Western media, many of them come from African journalists. But African journalists should bear one thing in mind – there are two sides to a story... If you are an African journalist and you do not see the beautiful side of Africa, you only see the bad and write negative things, then you are not being responsible.'

One of the ugly sides of Africa is the corruption that stalks Dar es Salaam and scores of capitals across Africa. Mengi believes that Africans are afraid to speak out about corruption for fear that they may lose contracts and alienate their contacts. In 2005, he started two newspapers in Tanzania to investigate the corruption that he believes is making the poor even poorer.

One of Mengi's favourite hobby horses is the Democratic Republic of Congo, which has an estimated $24 trillion in mineral wealth, yet its people go hungry.

'Africans are selling themselves too cheaply. When we encounter foreign investors, you talk of a deal for a gold mine. We think the deal is $1 million, they believe it is $100 million. Do you think they are going to say, "Why not make it $50 million or even $100 million?" They capitalise on our ignorance.'

In his own backyard, Mengi has invested millions in trying to create opportunities for his countrymen to benefit financially from Tanzania's vast oil and gas resources.

He has also poured millions into philanthropy through health and education. Along the way, he earned the nickname the 'Condom King' for his evangelical zeal in propagating the use of rubber.

'If you see someone on the roof of a house and think he's not all right and wants to jump down, and by jumping down he is going to die, but there is a ladder nearby, would you take the ladder and put it there for him to come down safely? Or would you say, "Just jump, just jump!"?' Mengi asks, stretching his homespun idiom to the max. 'I had a very big fight with the bishops in the Catholic Church. They said Mengi has a huge plant for making condoms ... Mengi is in collaboration with white people, he wants to use condoms to exterminate the black race.'

Far from it; Mengi wants to donate his wealth to help his fellow Africans flourish before he dies. There is a bit less of it in 2016, as the economy has not been kind to the Mengi fortune. His IPP Group, one of the largest conglomerates in Tanzania, is involved in both media and mining. The devaluation of the Tanzanian shilling, falling commodity prices and weak advertising sales have resulted in his fortune decreasing to a low of $300 million, according to estimates.

But Mengi still jets around the world and spends a lot of time with his family, of whom he is fiercely protective. He hardly ever speaks about them to the media. He is married to former singer and Miss Tanzania 2000, Jacqueline Ntuyabaliwe-Mengi, and they have two children.

In Tanzania, Mengi is considered a hard worker who is modest about his wealth. Mengi himself says his reputation is his most treasured possession, and that he takes everything as it comes with his trademark down-to-earth philosophy.

'Am I working harder than the poor woman cleaning the streets in the sun? Am I working harder than someone breaking stones at a construction site?' he asks rhetorically.

In these troubled economic times, many people can relate to his story of entrepreneurial triumph over poverty: from running around barefoot and sharing a hut with livestock to dining in the finest restaurants in Paris …

Mengi is living proof that, in Africa, anything is possible.

10

How the mouse ate the elephant

Stephen Saad

Stephen Saad

A FORMER AUDITOR WHO became a millionaire at 29 and a billionaire at 50, and who, in 2017, is worth $1.1 billion, according to *Forbes*: not too bad for a Durban boy who operates out of the seaside city of his birth and comes across as more beach than boardroom.

One could easily observe those two sides of Stephen Saad under his shock of grey hair and in his self-deprecating demeanour as he collected a trophy at CNBC Africa's prestigious All Africa Business Leaders Awards in September 2016.

His down-home lifestyle is his way of dealing with the stresses and strains of big business and being a billionaire. One wouldn't look twice at this Joe Soap from KwaZulu-Natal if you saw him in shorts, kicking a ball around with his kids on a Durban beach. He is a family man through and through, who likes to be at home or on his game reserve with the people he calls his 'big five': his wife and four daughters. One of the jokes in the pharmaceutical industry is that if you want to pitch a business deal to Saad, you had better book an airline ticket to Durban.

'I have a video-conferencing facility,' Saad says drily when asked why he rarely ventures far from KZN. In fact, he is well-travelled, but he leans on his home-town pride like a staff.

'I'm a Durban boy!' Saad smiles from the stage as he surveys the VIP audience below the bright lights of the awards ceremony.

During the 90 seconds he spoke, he recalled the little house-cum-office in Greyville, Durban, where he began his journey to untold wealth with a little company called Aspen.

'Not too far from the final post at the Durban July,' he says of its proximity to the famous racecourse. This was the humble beginning of Saad's life as an entrepreneur, in an old house with a washing line out the back.

In 2017, Saad runs a company valued at more than R200 billion; it listed on the JSE at 53 cents a share – today, it is at R300 a share. The company encompasses everything from pharmaceuticals to education – it seems that Saad can spot any gap in the market and plug it for a profit.

On the night of the awards, as he was being congratulated by an admiring crowd, Saad was eager, as always, to talk about his business. He advised everyone to fasten their seatbelts, because the best years for Aspen still lay ahead.

'To build a company in what was considered an industry that belonged to the developed world and to watch the FDA [Federal Drug Agency] and highly stringent regulators walk through our facilities, and the way our teams from New Brighton [near Port Elizabeth] work with absolute passion and these people turn around and say, "Wow, look at these people from South Africa." They thought they were coming to a game farm but they were coming to one of the top pharmaceutical companies in the world. It is those guys from the township that they are questioning and it is those guys who have got the skills to match anyone in the world.

'You know, my peers are saying that they are not investing because the political climate is not right, because the economic climate is not right. They are going to wait until Jesus comes! But I am telling you now – it is not going to happen. If you invest, you will create jobs and a working nation that is a happy nation. You won't have to worry about what the ratings agencies say – we can rate ourselves!'

Saad has always been driven by hope, but it is his keen eye for a business opportunity and his iron resolve to see a venture through that have been the keys to his success. But it could all have come to naught if it wasn't for an eye-opening stroke of luck when he was a young man.

Saad had initially walked a conventional path. He obtained an accountancy degree from the University of KwaZulu-Natal in Durban, played rugby in his spare time and joined Coopers & Lybrand as an articled clerk. It could have been a comfortable life for a man who wished to stay in Durban forever. And it was a career choice that had been expected of him.

'My father wanted me to extend the 30 years of family tradition by joining his practice, but I absolutely knew that there was no way that was going to happen. I couldn't do it. One of the partners at the time recognised this and privately told me that he could see that I was like a bird with its wings clipped.'

For Saad it was a sign to make a radical change, and it led to a stroke of luck that would change his fortunes. For many successful entrepreneurs, a bit of good luck is as important as planning, courage and determination. The most fascinating thing about it is that at the time, the entrepreneur has no idea how much his or her life is going to change. The key is to spot the opportunity and grab it with both hands.

So it was when the owner of a small company called QuickMed, which specialised in pharmaceutical wholesaling, was impressed by the young, free-spirited Saad and offered him a job.

Then in his late 20s and full of enthusiasm, Saad headed off to become a pharmaceutical rep in the townships. In those dim days of apartheid, this was not an easy task. The townships were riven by political violence and were seen as no-go areas for whites.

As Saad recalls, 'It was the 1980s, and tensions were running high. I had attended a school where there were only white people; it was a real eye-opener for me.'

Nearly a quarter of a century later, Saad looks back on his experiences in the townships as an integral part of his learning curve as an entrepreneur. There were many hairy moments along the way, including when he was hijacked on London Road, which runs through the sprawling Alexandra township in Joburg. It is just a hop, skip and a jump away from the glass towers of the wealthy business district of Sandton.

'We sold to markets and to people that other companies ignored. It was an eye-opener,' he repeats. 'Not many whites had ever been to a township, let alone done business there. But this was where the huge potential was. I was a rep in the townships and I learnt a lot of life lessons in those days. My future thinking was shaped in those early days.'

Selling in the townships taught Saad a salutary and invaluable lesson in the business that was to make his fortune: that although people were sensitive to the price of medicine, they were very reluctant to compromise when it came to their health. They were prepared to pay whatever it cost.

In the *Forbes Africa* interview with Saad, we talk about those early days, and for the first few minutes he is noticeably uncomfortable. He is clearly suspicious of having his thoughts probed by a stranger, but as the conversation moves to subjects that interest him, he relaxes and quite happily holds forth.

'When I was a rep, I was in the surgery of a township doctor and I presented him with two products. One was in fancy packaging and the other in a rather plain brown box. I suggested that he could give the first to his medical-aid patient and the other to his cash customers; after all, the products were essentially the same and were based on the same active ingredient. He looked me in the eye and told me that a patient is sick no matter what his or her status, and that he wouldn't treat them differently. He'd made his point, and I never forgot that.'

Those few sentences in a township surgery would change Saad's life and motivate him to become one of the wealthiest people in Africa. What he learnt that day was that there was an untapped, unmeasured and growing market that existed outside of the formal economy – a market that most of the white-run businesses ignored. It would be at their own expense.

When Saad became a 50 per cent shareholder at QuickMed, he convinced his employers that by owning the intellectual property, they could not only save the business, but grow it. He then set about dispensing the spirit of entrepreneurship that was to become the hallmark of everything he's done since.

One of QuickMed's early moves was to persuade Covan, a small, family-run business that manufactured eye drops, to merge with QuickMed to form a new entity called Covan Zurich. The company flourished in the early 1990s, and Saad threw himself into the business. They soon doubled their turnover, and suddenly the company became the focus of attention of larger companies. Prempharm (today Adcock Ingram) couldn't resist the little upstart and bought Covan Zurich for R75 million ($9.1 million) in 1993.

With the purchase, a restraint of trade was placed on Saad. He wasn't too worried at the time, as he had R20 million (about $2.4 million then) in his back pocket. At the age of 29, with thoughts of early retirement, a restraint of trade was a small price to pay. He thought he could use the time to reflect and plan for the future.

Although Saad still felt passionate about the pharmaceutical industry, education was also close to his heart, and that was where he launched his first solo venture.

Varsity College was a private tertiary institution that was being poorly managed and under threat of closure. Saad was offered the idea of turning the college into a business opportunity, and he teamed up with a colleague from QuickMed, Gus Attridge, to acquire the college with high hopes and at a nominal sum. Gus, an accountant whose real name is Michael – Gus is a nickname from his schooldays – is a family man like Saad who tries not to take work home. Today, Saad and Attridge, two friends from Durban, are worth $2 billion, almost as much as the annual budget of the seaside city where they were born.

At Varsity College, they set about restructuring the top-heavy overhead base, removed the founders and offered incentives to learners via aggressive advertising campaigns not normally seen in the conservative world of education.

'We placed adverts in the press,' recalls Attridge, 'centred around the F-word. It was actually F for fail, but it provoked some reaction, because it was a bit provocative, I suppose.'

Potential students and, more importantly, their parents, were offered a money-back guarantee should the students not pass their exams, provided they attended a full programme of lectures.

The business thrived. Within a paltry three years, Saad and his partners had turned a doomed college into a huge success. It had cost Saad and Attridge a mere R1.5 million ($182 500) to purchase, and they would sell it to LeisureNet for around R100 million ($12.1 million) at a time when education stocks on the JSE were attracting significant premiums to the overall market.

Flushed with success, Saad and Attridge then teamed up with Steve Sturlese to form Aspen Healthcare (Pty) Ltd. It was the humblest of beginnings, in an old Victorian house in Greyville, a short gallop from the Durban racecourse.

'It was in a rather less fashionable part of Durban. At the time, this was sugar cane,' says Attridge, sitting in Aspen's current, plush offices in the far trendier La Lucia.

The first days of Aspen's existence is seared into Saad's memory.

'I remember it well. Imported stock from Europe that was meant to arrive couldn't clear customs, and we had to have an emergency conference. That conference lasted three days and, after about 10 days, when we were discussing team-building exercises and action cricket, the stock arrived and I had to kick all the reps out onto the road to go and sell. So I will never forget the first days of Aspen; it was a bit of a disaster,' he laughs.

He continues: 'When I look back at the early days of Aspen, my philosophy was based on the experiences gained during my days as a rep and partner at QuickMed. In those days, I'd asked whether the business was about moving boxes or owning intellectual property. It was so obvious that there was a market out there that was hungry for high-quality but affordable products and that needed representation. Although this knowledge had been acquired through the little sphere of doctors that I serviced, I was convinced it could be applied on a bigger platform – even globally.'

His hunch was borne out at Aspen. In its first year of trading, Aspen recorded revenue of R105 million ($12.8 million). Its philosophy was clear from the start: buy licences from large multinationals for their non-core brands. These products were important to a new company selling to a new market. It was a mutually beneficial arrangement: the customers were ready to buy medication they had never been offered before, and the big players were happy to off-load them.

Aspen steadily gathered its own store of intellectual property, such as patents, trademarks and pharmaceutical dossiers, without having large overheads or taking on the risk of manufacturing with all its attendant complications.

Management quickly realised that they had a winning formula, but their ambitions were such that there was a real danger of running out of capital to back their plans.

To rectify this and pave the way for the grand plan, Aspen targeted Medhold Medical Ltd, a small company listed on the JSE.

Aspen concluded a reverse takeover of the business and thus became a public company. Records show that at the end of June 1998, Aspen's annual turnover was just under R119 million ($14.4 million). A year later, it had increased to more than R522 million ($63.5 million), and the investment community took note: the company's stock was on the move.

Then the audacious deal that would define the Aspen approach was unveiled. SA Druggists (SAD) had been the object of desire of giants Adcock Ingram, but that deal had fallen through. Despite the mismatch in terms of size, Saad approached his financiers with his plan to purchase SAD for the princely sum of R2.4 billion ($292.2 million). He worked hard to earn the backing of big-hitting financiers like property developer Jonathan Beare, who relishes backing small businesses (as Aspen was then), and Investec's chief executive, Stephen Koseff.

After many a slip – including a radio news bulletin announcing that the deal was dead – the SAD takeover was concluded. Fedsure was SAD's largest shareholder at the time, and they retained the insurance side and would manage the healthcare part of the business, while Aspen retained the pharmaceutical business. Once all the transactions were rubber-stamped, Aspen realised approximately R1 billion ($121.8 million) from the divestments.

Although the financiers had backed the upstart Aspen, there was institutional investor reticence to the deal, which seemed to defy conventional business logic. Aspen's bank asked that shares in Aspen be discounted, but this was not an option for Saad, and so the company was saddled with R1 billion in debt with an operating profit of around R123 million ($14.9 million).

'We didn't think we were going to buy the whole pharmaceutical business. I don't know whether it was fate, or what, but we got it,' recalls Attridge.

It was far from an easy marriage as a small management team at Aspen prepared to manage a giant like SAD from a small Victorian house in Greyville. The newspapers called it a mouse trying to eat an elephant – a Durban firm with a staff of 200 taking over a firm of around 3000 employees.

As Attridge recalls, 'The company, which we still own today, Pharmacare Limited, was a company within the SAD label that housed the pharmaceutical business, and we invited the chief executive of that business to come to Durban and meet with us to talk about our plans and strategies and to get to know him a little better. I think he took one look at that house, and the day after he handed in his resignation. I think he thought, "No, look at me in my office park with a view of a Johannesburg golf course, and these guys are sitting here looking into the backyard of someone with a washing line."'

The SAD deal proved a watershed. The story of Aspen has been one of extraordinary growth, and strategic agreements have been key to their expansion, not least the 2003 link with GlaxoSmithKline (GSK), which allowed Aspen to market and distribute 40 branded products into the South African private sector. During these deals, it is in the trenches that Saad shows his worth as an officer, pistol in hand, leading his men over the top. Working for him is clearly not for the faint-hearted.

The billionaire becomes animated when he tells the following story.

'I decided to bring all our people together from all our offices, from all over the world. So, of course, I chose Umhlanga Rocks for our conference. I stood in front of this group and told them that certain things were non-negotiable. They must have a passion for the business, and then people will follow them. At the same time, I told them that it was essential to have humility and compassion, and that there was absolutely no negotiation when it comes to delivery. In business, you get leaders and you get managers, and there's a very subtle distinction between the two. I want leaders; leaders are inspirational.'

Saad demands a lot of his employees, and he knows that as the head of the company and its inspiration, his behaviour and standards can never slip. When asked about his ability to maintain such a punishing pace, his stock response is: 'To rest is to rust.'

Despite his yearning for hearth and home in Durban, Saad is always on the move, visiting his 70 operations around the world. The international side to Aspen has made the company a good rand hedge, because more than half of its earnings come in hard currency from overseas. The company supplies medicine to more than 150 countries, manufactured at 16 sites across Kenya, Tanzania, Australia, Mexico, Brazil, Germany, South Africa, France, the Netherlands and the United States. That means serious flying time for Saad.

'I tend not to spend too much time at airports, as I usually arrive with a boarding card and only ever take hand luggage. I try and stay patient and see how many emails I can knock off,' he says.

China is one of his new destinations as Aspen tries to carve out a place in one of the world's biggest markets.

'China is a difficult terrain for all. Everything is not always apparent, and understanding cultural differences is critical. It may be a little easier, as an African, as we tend to be more accommodating and understanding of others. Given the population, their growing affluence and their desire for quality, affordable medicines, we simply have to be in China,' says Saad, for whom no challenge is too big.

'We were told that we were mad to manufacture in South Africa. Some analyst asked me if I was doing this for my own ego. I pointed out as politely as I could that I was a shareholder and that it was the right thing to do. Today, I'm so proud to be able to have proved the doomsayers wrong. Today, the billions [of rands] we invested in the Eastern Cape have produced one of the most competitive facilities in the world, which sends products of incredible quality to over 100 countries. It's up there with the very best.'

On the one hand, Saad is a man who is driven by the old-fashioned values of integrity and hard work and has stuck to a time-honoured way of doing business. On the other, he is a New Age thinker who recognises that big business is built on layers of bureaucracy and structures, but will not allow it to shelter slackers.

'At Aspen, I do not tolerate a "cover-your-arse" mentality,' he says with a hint of steely menace.

Then there's the affable CEO who is bursting with optimism for Africa and South Africa. He likes to compare the high suicide rates of northern Europeans, who seemingly have every material advantage, to those of optimistic African people who, in relative terms, have so little.

Saad says he'd rather back a good leader in a bad industry than a bad leader in a thriving industry. Might he, in his own diplomatic way (and in the presence of a *Forbes Africa* journalist), be taking a dig at the South African government?

When Saad talks about money, his enthusiasm wanes. He mutters that for most of the entrepreneurs he knows, money alone is not the motivating force.

'I still have lots of challenges that I need to focus on. It's so frustrating living in a country where there's great thought and great theory, great principles, but so little action. Maybe it's my personality type, but I just want people to stop thinking about a thing and just do it.'

Twenty years after the launch of Aspen, 2017 promises to be a big year for the company. It has consolidated its entry into the anaesthetics market and the forecasts are looking good. When the company built a sterile manufacturing and distribution network, the anaesthetics business became a good fit.

'Given the regulatory environment that exists within the global pharmaceutical business, it's hard to believe what we have achieved over the last three years. Indeed, our forecast looks great and we expect acceleration in H2 of 2017. So it's exciting times, but as with everything in life, the table is set but delivery will depend on execution,' Saad says.

Saad appears unlikely to start 'rusting' anytime soon, even after more than 30 years since his light-bulb moment in the townships.

'I have never forgotten my roots and never will,' he says firmly. 'Valuable life lessons and true humility are learnt and reinforced. This has profoundly shaped my thinking and personal philosophies regarding healthcare. The desperate need is better understood when you see it as opposed to reading about it. I have been privileged to be able to be part of a business that can contribute to our society and grow African people in an industry that was seen as a preserve of the developed world.

'They are right at the apex and we intend growing off this solid base. It's what keeps us motivated every day. And it means there is never, ever place for the rust to settle!'

11

The king of diamonds

Nicky Oppenheimer

Nicky Oppenheimer

T O SAY THAT Nicky Oppenheimer is understated is an under-
statement in itself. It is tantamount to saying that his family – the
third richest in Africa and worth an estimated $7 billion, according to
Forbes – is well-off; or that Winston Churchill, another famous Old
Harrovian, was a fair public speaker.

It must be tough to suffer the scrutiny that one invites as the scion of
a powerful, world-famous family, but Oppenheimer wears his eminence
lightly as he sits opposite me for this rare interview. His Johannesburg
office may be lavishly decorated, but the man himself, in a blue open-
necked shirt, is not. He is measured, calm and guarded as he chats about
everything from entrepreneurs and corruption to government and
business. Although he is hard to read behind his bushy grey beard, he
is gentlemanly to a fault.

And he is quietly proud when, at the end of the interview, he fleetingly
mentions his son's first-class cricket career as an Oxford blue. When
Jonathan Oppenheimer bowled for Combined Universities, he came
up against one of the world's finest batsmen, West Indian Brian Lara.

'He bowled the first three balls and moved them away and then
brought one back into the pad. Lara LBW, Oppenheimer 0,' chuckles
the proud father.

Oppenheimer's laid-back demeanour belies a busy few years for his
family and the two corporate giants that it took generations to build:
Anglo American and De Beers. In the foreseeable future, the Oppenheimer family will invest billions in Africa and its entrepreneurs. Their
new business philosophy is 'Out with diamonds and in with investing
in African entrepreneurs'. This is a whole new world for the distinctly
old-world Oppenheimers, as they look to blaze an investment trail
across the continent.

'You have to learn to get on with people,' says Oppenheimer from his armchair. 'You have to learn to separate the bullshit from the serious stuff, and then you have to have good common sense and a vision of where you want to get to.'

This no-nonsense approach is driving the family forward in the private-equity business. If they get it right, the family fortune is likely to increase along with the prospects of scores of African entrepreneurs from Cape Town to Addis Ababa.

The Oppenheimers' investment drive originated when they sold De Beers, the largest diamond producer in the world and a company the family had nurtured for nearly a century, to Anglo American for $5.1 billion in 2011. Although the Oppenheimers had founded Anglo American, they had long relinquished any control over the company. De Beers may have survived political upheaval and two world wars, but the recession of 2008 proved too much for the company.

'From a De Beers perspective, [the recession] came at a bad time,' recalls Oppenheimer. '[The company] had just been opening new mines, so we had to borrow money to pay for them. You don't get a return very quickly. So we had to renegotiate our debt conversion with the bank. That wasn't easy, but we managed. We had to turn to our share-holders and ask them for more money; this was post-privatisation. So both Anglo and the family put up more money, which was brave on everyone's part.

'My father used to talk about the Great Depression, where the situation was far more dramatic than anything I've ever had to face. [With the recession], you knew people still wanted to buy diamonds – there was never less of a desire for them – but they just didn't have the income to do it. So you had to cut your cloth to fit the suit and wait for the situation to improve … It never occurred to me that the business wouldn't recover; there were times where you had sleepless nights.'

So the heart-wrenching decision was made in 2011 when, after 85 years, the Oppenheimers voted to sell their 40 per cent stake in De Beers, the business on which the family fortune was built.

'It wasn't that difficult a decision,' Oppenheimer says now, with the benefit of hindsight. 'The fact that there were three shareholders in De Beers – the family, Anglo and the Botswana government – was always an unstable arrangement in my view, and I knew that something would happen at some stage. Either Anglo would say De Beers was not a business for them, or they would say that they really wanted to be in it, but in a much more serious way, and Anglo came out on that side and made us a very fair and reasonable offer.

'And then, of course, I was in a difficult position, because I had to deal with a business I had been in all my life on the one hand, and then the requirements of the family, my sister, her children, my children. We ended up in a situation where my heart said, "Look, we should stay with De Beers," but my head knew absolutely that this was the right deal to do.'

Analysts in Johannesburg say Mary Slack, Oppenheimer's sister, was a persuasive voice in the decision to sell. If it had not been for her, the family would not have sold, they say.

'She [my sister] was not in the day-to-day running of the business,' Oppenheimer says curtly. 'We all ended up wanting to sell.'

Selling De Beers broke a link that dates back to Nicky's grandfather, EO, or Ernest, who was born in Friedberg, Germany, the son of a cigar merchant. Ernest began his working life at the age of 17, when he started employment at Dunkelsbuhler & Company, a diamond brokerage in London. His efforts impressed his employer enough to post the 22-year-old to Africa.

Ernest arrived at the chaotic and dusty diamond diggings in Kimberley in South Africa's Northern Cape on a hot day in November 1902, with £50 in his pocket. Apparently he was a shy and diffident young man who struggled to break into Kimberley's close-knit, patriarchal society as an outsider with a German-sounding name. In British colonial Africa, such things were frowned upon.

A crucial moment in the young Oppenheimer's life occurred on the day he met the Member of Parliament for Kimberley, Leander Starr Jameson, a Scottish doctor and adventurer. He was the right-hand man of arch-colonialist Cecil John Rhodes, another Kimberley diamond digger, and had led an ill-fated coup attempt to overthrow the Boer government in Johannesburg in 1895 in what is known as the Jameson Raid.

Oppenheimer asked Jameson why his staff did not respect him, even though he worked longer than any of them sorting diamonds, according to Chris Ash's biography of Jameson, *The If Man*.

'Of course they don't respect you for working hard. Don't sort the diamonds; let them do the sorting,' Jameson told Ernest.

That is exactly what the young Oppenheimer did, while he concentrated on buying and selling the valuable stones, which was to form the basis of his fortune. It was said that he had an unparalleled knowledge of diamonds and carried a notebook around with him to jot down any useful business information.

By the time Ernest was 30, a mere four years after being elected to the city council, he became the mayor of Kimberley – no mean feat in an age when grey hair ruled the roost. He flourished in public life.

In 1921, the British government conferred a knighthood on Ernest, and three years later, he represented Kimberley in parliament as a member of the South African Party under General Jan Smuts. Oppenheimer was active in civil life and organised the labourers needed to build a railway line between Upington and the Namibian border. In his professional life, he founded Anglo American in 1917, and was elected in 1926 to the De Beers board, where he became a major shareholder.

'I always remember [Ernest] as a very quiet guy. I remember him as the sort of guy that if you bumped into him, you rebounded,' says his grandson more than a century later.

When Ernest passed away in 1957, he left his entire fortune to his son Harry, an outspoken young man who would make his mark both in business and politics. He would also maintain the family tradition of mentoring his son in the art of business.

Harry O, as he was known in the media, was educated in England at Charterhouse School in the leafy stockbroker belt of Surrey, where Boy Scouts founder Robert Baden-Powell was an old boy. He then enrolled at Christ Church, Oxford, graduating in 1931 in philosophy, politics and economics. By the age of 24 he was attending his father's board meetings back in Johannesburg, observing, listening and learning. Upon his father's death, Harry assumed leadership of the family business, and soon gained the reputation of being a tough nut. His son Nicky disagrees.

'No, I don't think he was a tough man in business. He knew the right way to get to a point and how to negotiate his way there. I would have thought my grandfather was a tougher businessman. I always knew that my father was there [for me] and that I could discuss business matters with him, and that gave me a head start. But it didn't get you to the finishing line; that was when you either delivered or not. He taught me that business was an assessment of risk and to be a successful businessman, you have to take risks. It is no good being risk averse; then you go nowhere.'

Nicky Oppenheimer's demeanour harks back to the gentility of the austere 1950s. A questionnaire-style interview conducted in 2011 by the South African publication *Mining Weekly* reveals a little of his unassuming, self-effacing character.

First Job: 'Bottlewasher' in the gold division of Anglo American.
Value of Assets under Your Control: I have no idea.
Number of People under Your Direct Leadership: About 10 000.
Management Style: That is something you should ask others about
– technical jargon of this kind is something I've been suspicious of.
Personal Best Achievement: Choosing my parents very well.

At the age of seven, Oppenheimer arrived in an austere post-war Britain, where ration books were still in force, to begin his prep-school education. He then went on to Harrow, like Winston Churchill, and Christ Church, Oxford, like his father.

'I am of an age where going to university was the last holiday of your life, and I thought that was absolutely fantastic. Politics, philosophy and economics were a good sort of all-round degree. I thought it was a fantastic, wonderful life. I didn't work very hard; I got a third-class degree at the end of it all. But I had a lot of fun,' Nicky recalls.

When he arrived home in South Africa in 1966, he was called up for compulsory national service. A couple of years earlier, Nelson Mandela and his comrades had been sentenced to life in prison for 'recruiting cadres for training ... in guerrilla warfare and acts of sabotage' (Wikipedia) in an attempt to overthrow the apartheid regime. Oppenheimer was drafted into this political maelstrom as a conscript, and earned his first pay packet, of 50 cents a day, in the process.

'The army had a terrible problem with me. I had a degree, and if you have a degree you did your basics and then became an officer. So I became an officer, and then they had no idea what to do with me. I had no skills that were of any use to them at all. I was sent to a great big parking lot just outside Pretoria, where I was required to sign my name every time a vehicle came in. I had to sign, saying that the vehicle had four tyres and two headlights. I always say that the army taught me how to sign my name very fast,' he smiles.

In 1968, after completing his military service, he became personal assistant to the chairman of Anglo American and took his seat on the board, which he was to occupy for 37 years.

'It is what I saw myself doing; I had a particular love for the Anglo business, the diamond business. So maybe that's historical, or whatever. I was lucky enough to achieve what any diamond person's primary ambition would be, and that's to become chairman of De Beers. I've been extraordinarily lucky.'

Not too soon after the De Beers exit in 2011, the E Oppenheimer & Son investment holding company and Temasek Holdings, a sovereign-wealth fund from Singapore, set up its investment arm, Tana Africa Capital, in a 50/50 partnership. Each put up $150 million, and sources say that the family is also ready to invest the billions they made from the De Beers deal. According to the company's website, 'The two like-minded investors were united by the common vision of creating value on the African continent through capital and business-building support. To date, the company has deployed more than US$250 million across the length and breadth of Africa.'

Tana Africa focuses its efforts on food, beverages and personal care, fast-moving consumer goods, retail and education, and will also consider select opportunities in healthcare, consumer financial services, media, logistics and agriculture.

'We are Africans, and we would like to invest in Africa,' says Nicky. 'So we are busy looking for things to do. We have some investments, but we are constantly on the lookout.'

Tana Africa has already invested in Promasidor Group, a company founded in the Democratic Republic of Congo in 1979, which sells everything from powdered milk to tea in 30 African countries, and has a minority interest in Regina, Egypt's second largest pasta manufacturer, which owns the country's only durum-wheat flour mill and has an expanding export business into Africa and the Middle East.

Oppenheimer has faith in African entrepreneurs. 'People are pretty entrepreneurial in Africa, and that is very encouraging. One constraint in Africa is bureaucracy. The problem lies in the fact that so many African economies are mineral-based. The thing with minerals is that you can't pick them up and take them anywhere, and that allows a government, wherever they are, to be bureaucratic, which is not business-friendly, because a business can't simply say, "I don't like you; I'm going to go somewhere else" – you've got to deal with it.

'As a continent, we've got to learn that you've got to be business-friendly and find ways to create an environment in which business can flourish. And that means a bit of a mind change. The important thing is that they [governments] have a huge role to play in controlling the environment. The less they have to do with the actual business, in my view, the better.'

Once again, I quote Ugandan president Yoweri Museveni, who said that it is easier for a camel to pass through the eye of a needle than it is to keep a government out of business.

Nicky replies, 'What one has got to realise, and what governments have got to understand, is that they are missing an opportunity. The penny will drop, and then they must do much more than you talked about. They have to create the right environment, they have to set the rules and regulations and tax rates, but the running of a business is something short term at which governments are really bad.'

And corruption?

'You have to stand up for what is right. Corruption is an extremely insidious and dangerous thing, and very difficult to eradicate once it starts ... I often ask people, once you've become a corrupt society, how do you stop being one? And you don't get many satisfactory answers. I think you have to demonstrate that you can be successful and contribute to society while being ethically sound, and it will be a long, slow process.'

'More legislation?' I venture as Oppenheimer appears to be opening up and warming to the conversation.

'I always worry about legislation and its consequences. Legislation is designed to catch the crooks. To my mind, the crooks are always too clever to be caught. What [corruption] does is make honest people's lives intolerable. So there has to be legislation, but there has to be a drive to get people to believe in business ethics and doing the right thing.'

Then there is the struggling mining industry, in which Oppenheimer worked for more than half his life. South Africa, once the mighty powerhouse of mining on the continent, has been shaken by strikes, power cuts and tinkering with mining laws. The Energy Intensive User Group (EIUG) of Southern Africa, which represents 32 of the area's biggest energy consumers – including the smelters and mines – announced that 97 per cent of its members were scaling down on capital projects because they feared potential power cuts.

'I think that people are looking at South Africa and waiting to see ...' Nicky says. 'That's a bad situation, as you don't want them to be in wait mode – you want them to be in invest mode. The key thing in South Africa seems to be the creation of jobs. The government's task, I think, should be to do everything in its power to create jobs so that the huge number of unemployed youth we have in this country can get jobs and fair, proper wages. That needs to inform every decision [government] makes.

'I think [government] has a huge contribution to make. People are talking about [minerals] like it's a curse, which it certainly isn't. Minerals have a future. If you are blessed with minerals, that's a fantastically good start – you've got to use them. I think what happened in Botswana is a good example of a country that has taken its diamond revenues and put them to good cause. You've got to find a way of encouraging mining, and mining is more long term than almost anything else.

'So you've got to create an environment in which somebody is going to invest billions of dollars with a view that the first return will be seven to 10 years away. And they believe that the deal they have and the environment they are dealing in will still be there in seven to 10 years' time. Then you will find people and companies who will invest …

'It is going to depend on the mining legislation, which is a bit up in the air at the moment. If you want to invest in a mine, you have to ask, "Am I confident that the environment that the government creates for me will stand the seven- to 10-year test?"'

Oppenheimer concedes that the battered image of mining in the land of his birth has made foreign investors think twice about staking any claims here.

In the next few years, the Oppenheimer family will be investing millions to ensure that more entrepreneurs are made and their employees paid fair and proper wages. It could lead to another colourful chapter in the history of one of the most famous families on the continent.

12

The immigrant priest who became a steel baron

Narendra Raval

Narendra Raval

I N KENYA, THEY call him Guru, which in Sanskrit means 'teacher', 'leader' or 'master'. And Narendra Raval must surely be one of *the* unlikeliest multimillionaire entrepreneurs in Africa. In 1978, at the age of just 16, Raval arrived in Africa with little more than the clothes on his back, to serve as a priest at the Swaminarayan Temple in Nairobi. But he soon proved that he was mature for his age, having been a priest's assistant back home in India from the age of 11, when he pioneered a counselling service for those of his peers struggling with drug abuse.

Nearly 40 years later, Raval – palm reader, astrologer and priest – is worth $400 million, according to *Forbes*, and flies to work in his own helicopter. Even he could not have foretold what lay in store for him in Kenya. His success is the result of many a long day's slog, resilience, a knack for spotting an opportunity and the humility to scrape his way up from the very bottom. Raval is a monopoly breaker who is always ready to take a million-dollar risk to disrupt the market and get what he wants. Complacency is not in his vocabulary.

Raval is partial to dark suits and red ties, which he wears to the boardroom where he counsels high-ranking politicians and business people as he presides over his baby, Devki Companies, a conglomerate that employs more than 4000 people. Devki manufactures steel, cement and sheet roofing, and, according to *Forbes*, generates revenue of at least $650 million a year.

None of this would have been possible without Raval's wife Neeta, whom he was pressurised into marrying as a young man, as his father thought it would set a good example to his two younger siblings.

'My family forced me to get married,' he says.

No one could have known it at the time, but the match would launch the former priest on his way to riches. But it was painful at first. In 1982,

Raval had to leave the temple because of the impending nuptials, and he married Neeta three years later.

The following year, the newlyweds tried their hand at business. They opened a hardware shop called The Steel Centre in one of Nairobi's bustling downtown areas, known as Gikomba, where the famous market sells the cheapest clothes in the land. In May 2014, an explosion – believed to have been set off by Islamic militants – rocked the market, killing at least 12 people and injuring 70. It was just one of many bomb attacks Nairobi has suffered in the last two decades.

Raval and his wife were tempted to the lean streets of Gikomba when a former Kenyan finance minister – one of Raval's many political connections he had made through his wise counsel as a guru – offered them a sweetheart deal. The minister owned a small shop, which he offered to the couple for a mere $70 a month in rent, about a quarter of the amount the couple would have paid in the smarter end of town.

'My wife and I did everything ourselves,' Raval remembers. 'One of us would make the deliveries, while the other manned the shop.'

The risk paid off. The Steel Centre was soon making $24 000 a month, says Raval – a pretty penny in 1986.

Raval stockpiled the capital in preparation for a much bigger venture – one that would make his fortune. He decided to become a steel manufacturer. It was a risky business in Africa, but it promised millions if it paid off.

Again, it was his well-nurtured political connections that stood him in good stead. One of Raval's acquaintances was former Kenyan president Daniel arap Moi, who promised to help set up Raval's steel factory, provided the company employed Kenyans before anyone else. Some of Moi's friends offered to sell Raval land, but it was too dear for his pocket.

In 1989, plans gathered pace when Raval secured 30 acres in Athi River, a vast industrial zone about 35 kilometres south of Nairobi. It came cheaply, too – about $4 000 for the lot. Nearly 30 years on, this amount of money will barely buy you a fraction of an acre around Nairobi.

Raval's tract of land didn't look much like an industrial zone at the time, and the nascent steel company had to share it with wild animals. This was the feral birthplace of Devki Steel.

'It was a piece of land that hid any potential it had away from us,' recalls Raval.

The Kenya Commercial Bank, a government-owned institution, lent Raval $700 000 to build the factory, import raw materials and kick-start production by 1992.

From the beginning, it was tough going. The business had very little cash flow, and the three big steel manufacturers of East Africa tried to eradicate Devki Steel from the outset by unleashing a price war. If Devki Steel sold their product for $10, the competition would offer it for $9. The established companies would also negotiate with suppliers to bring down the price of their raw materials.

'They priced their products a few shillings below ours,' Raval says. 'They had established markets, so their dubious pricing tactics did not affect their bottom line.'

Six months after commissioning the plant, Devki Steel was selling less than 10 per cent of what it was producing; inside the factory was a growing mountain of unsold and raw materials.

'I was almost on my knees,' Raval told the website Jozi Gist in 2015. 'No one was buying our products, because they could get it at a cheaper price from our competitors. We had tons and tons of raw materials and finished products just taking up space in our warehouse. It was a nightmare.'

To make matters worse, Raval had to freeze the salaries of his Kenyan employees. After explaining the situation to his workers, they agreed to go without a salary for a period of three months; Raval gave them only a small allowance for food.

'There were about 60 of them at the time. But they were very understanding. They said to me: "Guru, don't worry. We know the problem. We will work for you; don't give us a full salary – just give us enough to run our house. Give us the rest when you've made money." I used to work with them directly in the factory. We were a small company, so

I didn't have time to be the boss and spend the whole day in a fancy office. I was working *with* them – operating machinery, getting my hands dirty every day.

'My wife used to drive the truck and deliver our products to clients. So we interacted a lot with our workers on an informal level, talking about family, sports and other things. We never once saw them as workers – we were family. And in that spirit, they were very accommodating and understanding. They all stayed with us throughout those dark times.'

Just when all hope appeared to have evaporated, a stroke of luck befell Kenya from the international steel markets. The third quarter of 1992 ushered in a steel shortage and international prices skyrocketed. All of a sudden traders were prepared to pay anything to get their hands on as much steel as they could. Prices soared from $300 to $600 per ton within a month.

Devki Steel was in the pound seats. Its warehouses were full: they had $1.2 million worth of finished steel and raw materials. Raval made a killing almost overnight: $1 million in profit. Devki Steel was in business.

'The profit enabled me to settle my workers' dues, clear my bank loan and invest in expanding the factory,' recalls Raval, as he shakes his head in disbelief at his good luck.

Devki Steel would go from strength to strength across the entire East African region. Seventy per cent of its steel products are sold at home in Kenya, and the rest is exported to Rwanda, Uganda, South Sudan, Tanzania, Burundi and Ethiopia.

The rising prices of 1992 launched Devki Steel into the future. At the time, the company produced a mere 7 500 tons of steel reinforcement bars and tubes. By 2015, it was making 250 000 tons of more than 100 different finished products.

Now in his mid-50s, Raval is far from ready to take his foot off the gas. In 2008, he borrowed $72 million from his steel business to buy Maisha Mabati Mills, opposite the train station in Ruiru, a short drive north-east of Nairobi. Here he manufactures aluminium and zinc-coated iron sheets to roof the homes of lower-income Kenyans.

Since it was established, the company has grown its assets to more than $125 million; it churns out 200 000 tons of metal products every year.

In 2010, it was cement. Raval sank $100 million into building National Cement, which started out with a single grinding mill that turned out 350 000 tons of cement a year. Investment has increased the grinding capacity by five times and raised output to 1.2 million tons. By 2016, it had captured more than a fifth of the Kenyan cement market.

Raval's ventures caught the eye of the World Bank and its lending arm, the International Finance Corporation. In 2014, Raval accepted a $70-million package from the IFC: $55 million in debt and $15 million in return for a minority stake in the Devki Group. Raval considered it a boost for his adopted country at a time when the IFC estimated that Africa needed to increase cement production by between 10 and 15 million tons every year, for the next decade, merely to keep up with demand.

'We would like to send a strong signal of the IFC's confidence in a Kenyan company making a difference in the local economy,' Raval said when the deal was announced.

Raval used the IFC money to increase National Cement's production to two million tons by the end of 2016, and he built a clinker factory. The $200-million expansion will make National Cement the largest manufacturer in Kenya. It is part of Raval's ambition to be the biggest manufacturer of steel and cement in Africa.

Johnson Nderi, an analyst with ABC Capital in Nairobi, believes the increase in supply brought the price of a 50-kilogram bag of cement down from $9 to $7. 'Kenya has been experiencing a construction boom, and it is therefore logical that the monopolistic cement industry in the country has finally come to an end,' Nderi says.

By doing the deal with the IFC, Raval had gone where many entre-preneurs on the continent fear to tread: he rebuffed Africa's richest man, Aliko Dangote. Nigeria's billionaire cement king had wanted to buy Raval out, but then diluted his offer to a majority stake. Raval said no.

'We had our reasons for not accepting Dangote's offer,' Raval explains. 'The IFC, other than offering financial support, will also bring on board their expertise in infrastructure management.'

It is all part of Raval's big plan for Africa. By 2020, he aims to have set up steel and cement factories in the Democratic Republic of Congo, Uganda, Tanzania, Zambia and Nigeria at a cost of around $150 million, with support from the IFC.

Dangote tried to break into the Kenyan cement market on his own with a plant in Kitui County, but by late 2016 the project appears to have stalled. A Dangote-owned company, prospecting for limestone in the area, appears to have packed up and left. But reports in Kenya say that, for now, Dangote will import cement from his plants in neighbouring Ethiopia, with a plan to build a cement factory in Kenya by 2019.

Raval aims to list his company on the Nairobi Securities Exchange by 2020; it is his dream to give Kenyans a chance to own a part of his company. He also wants to be remembered as the man who gave every Kenyan a roof over their head without having to break the bank.

'I'm a spiritual man. I believe God helps people. But if you work hard and you persevere and remain good to people, the universe will reward you. Do not cheat your customers; always give them good-quality products and good prices,' he muses.

Like many of the billionaires in Africa, Raval tries to give back to society, donating much of his wealth and financially supporting thousands of people. When his employees retire, he gives them seed capital to start their own business. One of them runs a trading company that buys more than $1 million worth of goods from Devki Group every year.

Aside from all this, Raval is a trained pilot who choppers himself on his visits to his many factories. So, if you are ever in Nairobi and see a helicopter swooping overhead, it might just be a steel- and cement-making former priest on another money-making mission.

13

From cheap clothes to diamonds

Christo Wiese

Christo Wiese

C HRISTO WIESE IS the billionaire who is always on the move, never completely satisfied. He generates money like a silkworm secretes silk at a time of life when many billionaires would have long retired to their superyacht. It is what he does. He rarely fails to surprise the market with his long-term investments and strokes of luck. When he is not working, he is a voracious reader and television news junkie, where he searches for the next big deal.

Wiese's fortune is rooted in a simple idea: that people who don't have much money still want to look good. That idea transported him from a small town as a farmer's son to his current position as Africa's third richest man. Wiese is very careful with his money, to say the least; through recession and political upheaval, he has managed to gather lots of it. His is a tale of growth through acquisition blended with frugality.

His company boardroom at Pepkor Holdings overlooks not the magnificent Cape Town Waterfront or Table Mountain, but the far-from-glamorous Parow Industria on the fringes of Cape Town. Across the road there is a shoe factory and a company that sells compressors. This low-key location speaks volumes about Wiese and the way he does business.

Wiese likes to joke that the boardroom at his headquarters is bigger than his family's first clothing store, the font of his fortune. *Forbes*, in New York, called him Africa's Sam Walton, the founder of Walmart. Wiese calls himself Christo, and simplicity is his game; the clear-cut, forthright way he does business is also the way he lives his life.

Take the incident in 2009 when a customs official stopped him at Heathrow Airport and discovered a million dollars in cash neatly stacked in two briefcases. Customs confiscated the money and the case went to court.

Wiese's advocate argued that the million dollars was less than his client earned in a week. Wiese himself said he was flying to invest the money in Luxembourg.

'It's just peanuts to me' ran the headline in the *Daily Mail*.

The court ruled in the South African billionaire's favour and the money was returned – with interest.

'It's my money,' says the forthright billionaire. 'I didn't steal it from anybody. I didn't defraud anybody. It's my money and it is certainly my right to do with it as I please.'

On another occasion, when the press criticised his former CEO at Shoprite, Whitey Basson, for earning R82.7 million ($6.35 million) a year in a country where so many people earn only a minimum wage, Wiese countered that Basson was underpaid, taking into account the money he had made for shareholders. Wiese added modestly that the job was too big even for him. But he has no illusions about the envy of others.

'If you are positive about life, you ignore the unfair criticism. A lot of the criticism is totally justified, but you don't focus on the nice things people say to you, and equally you don't concern yourself too much about the bad things people say; they are often ill-informed on both sides. People might think that you are better than you really are, or they make negative comments that are not based on fact. I don't remember anything negative that people say. I always say to entrepreneurs, "If you start rising above the average, you become a target." People say, "But that guy is not cleverer than I am; why is he a success and I'm so clever and I don't make the same financial success?" You have to know that people will tear you down; it's part of the game,' he says philosophically.

Now in his mid-70s, Wiese shows few signs of slowing down. In 2016, he used his vast cash reserves to invest in a struggling industry in the belief that it can make him even wealthier. This is in addition to the $5.5 billion (according to *Forbes* in its African billionaire's list of 2017) he has accrued in his lifetime. Even so, the flagging diamond industry was a strange choice for a new venture.

The dominant player, Anglo American, which owns De Beers, reported a 19 per cent decline in rough-diamond output in the April–June quarter of 2016. Production had dropped by 31 per cent in Namibia, 26 per cent in South Africa and 12 per cent in Botswana.

Maybe the canny Wiese spotted a trend before deciding to invest his money. In the first half of 2016, sales figures reported an increase of 8 per cent in sales of cut diamonds, from $3 billion to $3.3 billion in the same period the year before.

On a pleasant spring morning in Cape Town, Wiese is looking relaxed in a pair of jeans and a black sweatshirt, en route to the airport for a flight to London to oversee his growing empire in Europe. So much to do elsewhere, so why the takeover bid in the African diamond industry?

'I used to be in the diamond industry 40 years ago, and the opportunity arose to acquire a controlling stake in Trans Hex, which is one of the junior diamond-mining companies, and one that I think has potential.'

Trans Hex is an alluvial diamond miner. In August 2016, Wiese bought 47.08 per cent of the company and, with investment outfit RECM and Calibre Limited, which own 25.2 per cent of Trans Hex, launched a mandatory offer for the whole company at R3.94 per share. The independent board of Trans Hex advised shareholders to hold out for more than twice that figure, but they sold anyway.

Trans Hex has operations in South Africa, and owns a 33 per cent stake in Somiluana mine in Angola and 40 per cent of West Coast Resources, which bought the Namaqualand mine from De Beers. The Angolan operations offset losses in the South African mines. Net profit for the six months to the end of September 2016 was R32.5 million.

'[The company] is doing well, except the exchange rate is not in favour of diamond exports because the rand is stagnant. With the diamond industry, you are not running a shop where you always know what your sales are going to be.'

Wiese sounds as sanguine as ever. Has he ever made a bad investment?

'Oh yes, plenty. I can't even remember the worst one, but there are many adventurous investments that just didn't work out. I am heavily invested in wine farming, and that's not a very lucrative business. But it offers other pleasures, such as its beauty. And you create potential tourism, because these places are exquisitely beautiful and people go there to enjoy the scenery, the history, the architectural beauty.'

Wiese has a wealth of experience in high finance on the world stage. It is a universe away from the tiny town of Upington – population 72 000 – from which he hails. Situated on the sweltering fringes of the Kalahari in South Africa's Northern Cape, Wiese and the tourism promoters of the provincial capital of the Northern Cape call it an oasis, due to its location on the banks of the Orange River.

The small town was founded as a mission station back in 1875, and by the 1880s it consisted of a disciplined, hard-working, dry-as-a-bone farming community. One of the legacies of the past is a statue of a donkey, harnessed to a water pump, in front of Upington Museum – a tribute to the beasts who sweated for the water that turned near desert into fertile land.

As the years went by, Upington became better known for having the longest tarred runway of any airport in the southern hemisphere – nearly five kilometres long – and for the fruit of its farmers, who coax world-famous grapes and raisins from the harsh, sun-baked soil.

Wiese's father was a sheep and cattle farmer. He proudly claims that his parents never worked for anyone. His mother was a woman of great wisdom and drive, he says, who raised a family and started her own businesses on the side.

'I grew up in a household where that was the way one approached life, which I found was of great benefit to me.'

Despite being the son of two entrepreneurs, Wiese took a more conservative approach when he sought a career. He spent the last two years of school at the prestigious Paarl Boys' High, then enrolled at the University of Cape Town. But he dropped out after a year and returned to Upington to join his father in business.

That could have been that, but the urge to achieve more was too strong. At the age of 21, Wiese left Upington and went to study law at the University of Stellenbosch. The university has been a finishing school for a generation of South Africa's finest and wealthiest entrepreneurs: billionaire Johann Rupert, media tycoon Koos Bekker, and investment wizards GT Ferreira and Jannie Mouton.

Back on a quiet Upington street, Wiese's parents and some family members co-founded PEP Stores in 1965 and they became its second largest shareholders. It was a humble beginning – a tiny shop that sold racks of clothes at knock-down prices. (In 2016, PEP opened its 2 000th store with a celebration in Cape Town.)

The business was founded on the principle that even lower-income people wanted to look good, in fashion they could afford. By selling bargain-bin clothing, the shop would make money no matter what the economic conditions. The business taught the young Wiese the value of high-volume, low-margin trade. It was the beginning of his love affair with the family firm that has lasted for more than half a century.

During the university holidays, Wiese would return to Upington to work for the company. He spent many days driving across the vast open expanses of South Africa locating spots for new stores, as the business was expanding rapidly.

'I travelled a lot, and I was often away from home for 20 days in a month, travelling, opening shops, visiting shops. The hours were way longer, but I was also younger,' he recalls.

Wiese graduated in 1967, and the pull of the family business proved stronger than law. He returned to work for the company as an administrator, doing whatever needed to be done. He was eager to learn the business, and was always observing, taking notes, acquiring knowledge.

Then, in 1973, the lure of law drew him back. Wiese left hearth and home to practise at the Cape Bar until 1979. It was also at about this time that he bought his first stake in the diamond business, in a mine near Upington, on a dry scrub of land around the Richtersveld. Wiese, a long-standing shareholder of PEP Stores by that time, bought the mine for around $20 million and sold it five years later, making enough profit to finance his next venture.

'Christo has been a massive risk-taker all his life,' says veteran

Johannesburg retail analyst Syd Vianello, who has studied Wiese for decades. 'Africa is not a place for sissies. You've got to have nerves of steel.'

In 1981, with his nerves tempered, Wiese made the investment that was to turn him into an entrepreneur for life. Brimming with ambition, he bought out his cousin, the founder of PEP Stores, for a tidy sum – about $100 million in today's money. The deal set his cousin up for life, and Wiese got a vibrant business in return. By this time, PEP Stores consisted of 450 shops and a grocery business, Shoprite, which it had bought for a million rand.

At the time PEP Stores acquired Shoprite, it had fewer than 500 employees and only eight stores. In 2012, its turnover was $9.5 billion; in 2016, it had more than 2000 stores across Africa and was the continent's largest food retailer, worth more than R100 billion. It bore out Wiese's three-point investment philosophy: returns, ethics and long term.

'The objective for people like myself is not to see how much money you can make, because there will always be somebody richer than you – so what the heck?' says Wiese. 'I often say that I know a lot of people who've made a lot of money in different businesses, with different formats, with different styles, but the one golden thread is that to make money takes decades.'

In 1982, Wiese changed the name of the group to Pepkor and got down to cutting costs. For a start, it acquired 11 factories and began manufacturing many of the clothes it sold. The company also set up a central distribution system and warehouses that cut down on truck deliveries and saved a fortune on overheads. It also opened as many as 100 stores a year and went on an acquisition spree at the right time, when the low-end fashion industry was booming.

Wiese's student friend at Stellenbosch University, billionaire Jannie Mouton, says, 'I think what's important is that [Christo] understands risk. He's not scared to take risks. He believes in himself and he will back [himself]. He's not scared to raise money for a good business proposition.'

Risks often loomed large. In 1985, Wiese experienced one of his toughest times in business. In that year, in just a few months, the rand collapsed and lost 50 per cent of its value against the US dollar. Pepkor, the holding company, bled money. Drastic times called for drastic measures.

'Well, you sit down with the team and regroup every time something bad happens and you fight your way out of it. All businesses do that, and all businesses should fight through crises,' Wiese says philosophically.

In order to take the strain off the balance sheet, Wiese was forced to restructure the entire company. Shoprite was listed separately, and many of Pepkor's non-core assets were sold off. The strategy worked. Within a year, Pepkor went from paying interest on debt of R140 million (about $10 million) to having about R110 million (about $8 million) in the bank.

Getting out of a tight corner, says Wiese, is a skill you learn only through experience.

'There is no secret, really. In this company, we have always had a philosophy in terms of which we run our group of companies. These are the five pillars, as we call it: faith, positive thinking, enthusiasm, compassion and hard work. Hard work is probably important, but you've got to be a positive person and able to put teams together and motivate them. I am not a person running the business; I play a different role. The good business leaders, like Whitey Basson [who stepped down in 2016] and Markus Jooste, are people who can put teams together, motivate them and steer them in the right direction,' Wiese says.

How does he choose his leaders for the rough times?

'It's more luck than wisdom. You try to gauge if the people live on the same planet, if they see life the same way you do, and you judge by that. In many instances, there have been friendships over decades and it just happened that we work together in business as well.'

Five years after the rand's collapse, the sun came out. In February 1990, after spending 27 years in incarceration, Nelson Mandela was released from prison. Democracy was on the way, and the world was opening up to South Africa, ending its pariah status and decades of sanctions.

The Wiese empire started stretching its legs on the African continent. Shoprite became the first of the stable of companies to set up shop outside South Africa when it moved into Zambia in 1994, buying out and rejuvenating the old government-owned OK Bazaars chain and drawing vast crowds of shoppers to Cairo Road in Lusaka, where cheap basic goods were in short supply. PEP Stores soon followed.

Wiese's stores did so well that in 1996 the Zambia Chamber of Commerce and Industry complained to the South African government that the flow of hard currency out of the country for imported goods was so strong, it was dragging down the value of the kwacha. I reported on that story at the time. The business elite of Zambia went so far as to invoke the days when their country sheltered ANC-affiliated guerrillas and protected them from cross-border raids. Couldn't South Africa protect Zambia against the marauding Shoprite? The story soon faded from the headlines and Shoprite kept on selling.

Wiese had realised before many of his peers that the new political dispensation in South Africa would result in international brands heading for the country's stores. He made the shrewd decision to take the competition to the rest of the world instead, and expanded into Europe, a move that has increased the company's profits to more than $2 billion.

The company launched in Europe in 1999. After 27 years on the JSE, Pepkor delisted, valued at $331.4 million, on the recommendation of the private equity company Brait, which claimed that Pepkor would prosper without having to endure the public scrutiny of its accounts. (Wiese is the top shareholder in Brait, with a 35 per cent stake.)

Through Brait, Wiese managed to snap up a number of big players in Europe. In June 2015, he bought a majority stake in British discount retailer New Look for $1.2 billion; a month later, he bought Richard Branson's fitness chain, Virgin Active, for $1 billion.

'It's a great business and a great investment,' Wiese says of the Virgin Active acquisition, 'and it ticked all the boxes that needed to be ticked before I invested. It is a business that has strong management, a proven track record and great growth potential, and management themselves have invested in the company.'

European expansion and diversification have helped Wiese ride out the sluggishness in the African economies. Even so, on the other side of the coin, Wiese admits that Brexit has hurt the share price a bit. Brait had ploughed £1.6 billion into Britain at just the wrong moment, as the country voted to leave the European Union. It was a move that hammered the pound, and Wiese's 35 per cent stake in Brait dropped by about $1 billion as a result.

Despite all of this, 'revenue' is still Wiese's middle name. In 2016, Shoprite brought in revenue of $9.9 billion; Pepkor's parent company, Steinhoff, which does business in Africa, Europe and Australasia, brought in $11.8 billion, selling everything from cellphones to sofas. The two companies between them employ 200 000 people in 9 000 stores in 30 countries.

While these results were coming in, Wiese was handing out house keys and title deeds to some of the underprivileged in Africa who had never owned a home before.

This initiative was launched by the Free Market Foundation (FMF), which encourages governments around the world to give people who are occupying land ownership of the property. In South Africa, the FMF found that there were between seven and 11 million households where the occupants owned the structure on the land, but not the land itself. The FMF subsequently joined forces with the provincial governments to launch an initiative whereby people can obtain full ownership of their properties.

'My family decided to get involved in [the initiative] via financial contributions so that people can acquire the title deeds to their homes,' Wiese says. 'It is an enormously important thing for people to have a sense of ownership. People who are used to owning things do not realise how much it adds to a person's dignity if he can say, "This is my home. It may be a modest little home, but it's my home and I can leave it to my children and be assured that they have a roof over their heads." It's very, very important.'

One person who benefitted from this philanthropy is 90-year-old Ngaungau Martha Olifant, who had waited a lifetime to own her own home. On a windy afternoon in Ngwathe Municipality in South Africa's Free State, she was one of 200 new homeowners who were handed a shiny new front-door key by one of the richest men in Africa.

When Olifant was born in South Africa in 1925, the ANC was a mere 12 years old.

'I was really afraid that I was going to die with nothing in my name after working so hard,' Olifant said in her mother tongue, Sotho, 'and that was a very painful thought for me. I used to earn R3 a week working in a factory and I managed to extend my rented house and furnish it, but it bothered me because I knew at any time I could be told to leave. I have been renting all these years.'

Wiese was the first to admit that the 200 front-door keys were a drop in the ocean in a country where seven million people need homes.

'I will certainly do everything I can to persuade not only the businesses that I'm involved in, but also other businesses, other institutions, organisations and individuals, to step up and help,' Wiese said that day in the Free State.

As Olifant looked up at the ceiling of her new home, she was sad that her husband, who had died 15 years before, did not get to see the day she took ownership of her own house.

Wiese believes that the young entrepreneurs of Africa can create enough wealth to provide homes for millions of homeless people. He has advice for young, ambitious entrepreneurs: 'I would point them to the five pillars of our philosophy. You have to have faith in yourself, in your country, in your fellow countrymen; if you are a religious person, have faith in a higher being. Always be positive; if you want to think of all the bad things in the world, you will do nothing, so think about positive things and approach everything positively.

'Be enthusiastic about what you are doing. If everything you do is a pain in the backside, then you are not going to get anywhere. Love what you are doing. Have compassion for other people, understand that their circumstances are different to yours and, finally, work your butt off. It's a simple formula.

'Success is about more than how much money you have. At the end of the day, I think it's about whether you can look at yourself in the mirror and say, maybe it's very small, but my contribution made life or the world a slightly better place. That's all. That's the measure of success.'

Christo Wiese: plain, simple and very, very successful.

14

Of wine, women and wrong

Wendy Appelbaum

Wendy Appelbaum

S HE IS ONE of the richest women in Africa, and is often portrayed as tough and ruthless, a businesswoman who takes no prisoners. And she can indeed be blunt, unafraid to use a few choice words to hammer home a point. An outspoken character who tears into chauvinists in the boardroom, she is also the thoughtful winemaker who plays gentle music to her prize-winning grapes.

'Men look at life differently,' Wendy Appelbaum claims. 'They are not as upfront and as honest as women. They compete in a relatively underhand way.' In business, Appelbaum pushes the cause of her gender tirelessly, in a spirit forged at her father's knee.

Feisty and cheeky, but also witty, bubbly and quick with a hug, people who know Appelbaum agree that she does have a heart, and that she is not afraid to wear it on her sleeve. These diverse personality traits have guided her most successful investments and made her millions in her own right, even though she was born into wealth.

Appelbaum, born and raised in South Africa, is vociferous on her favourite subjects: wine, women and wrong. She is not afraid to take anyone on, especially when it comes to her net worth, which *Forbes* estimated is as high as $183 million. 'Complete rubbish,' she says tersely. Other media organisations put the figure even higher; you can only imagine what she says to them.

'I don't think the point is how much you've got. The point is what you choose to do with it.'

Appelbaum's father, Sir Donald Gordon, cast a huge shadow across African business, and she was born under it. Gordon, who was knighted in 2005 for his charity work, was the doyen of the South African business world, and worth an estimated $1.6 billion (*Forbes*).

The Gordon family rose from rags to vast riches in just under a century. Arriving from Lithuania as empty-handed immigrants in the 1920s, they were among tens of thousands of Jews who sought a better life for themselves on African soil between the turn of the 19th century and the end of the 1920s, fleeing the rise of anti-Semitism in the Baltic States.

Many of the Lithuanian immigrants would make a name for themselves in the fast-growing cities of Johannesburg and Cape Town. Joe Slovo rose to become the head of the South African Communist Party; Albie Sachs became a Constitutional Court judge; Arthur Chaskalson was chief justice; and Johnny Clegg is one of South Africa's best-known activist musicians.

Appelbaum's grandfather, an accountant by trade, started on the bottom rung of the job ladder when he got to Johannesburg, working his heart out in a laundry to feed his family. Donald, born in 1930, knew only one thing as he grew up in those lean years: he wanted to make money. A bright child who dreamt of becoming a scientist, he instead settled for the safety of commerce as an auditor. This workaday career gave the young man his first business idea.

One day, while he was auditing an insurance company, he noticed that the firm was making a profit despite the fact that it was badly run. He thought he could do a lot better. In 1957, at the tender age of 27, he risked $120 000 to found a life insurance company. Liberty Life was to become a household name. When he sold the company to Standard Bank in 1999, it was worth more than $12 billion on the JSE.

An offshoot, London-listed Liberty International, launched in the shopping boom of the 1980s, would become one of the largest regional shopping-centre companies in Europe, consisting of a string of malls across Britain. It includes the Lakeside Shopping Centre in Thurrock, the MetroCentre in Gateshead and Braehead Shopping Centre in Glasgow. Gordon holds dual citizenship in South Africa and the UK, and a staff of eight looks after his investments. The man himself shuttles between homes in London, Florida and South Africa on his $45-million Falcon 7X jet.

Wendy Gordon grew up in a family where dinner-table conversation revolved around business and the entrepreneurial spirit. Every evening her father would come home with new business lessons, which he enthusiastically passed on to his daughter and sons, Richard and Graeme. Gordon taught them how to spot and maximise any opportunity, which would prove useful to Appelbaum, as she has spent her whole business life trying to prove to herself that she is more than just an heiress. Her father provided much of the know-how. 'My father had a wonderful way of verbalising what he was doing … It was like living in an MBA class.'

There is no doubt that Appelbaum greatly admires her father, but she is keenly aware that he is far from perfect. She knows her free business education came at a price.

'He wasn't interested in your opinion; he was interested in you as an audience. My father needed to be told how clever he was all the time. There was that need for affirmation, which most serious executives need. They really need their ego stroked. That's why, when you look at corporations, very often the succession is not there because they had a bunch of yes-men behind them, telling them that no matter what they did, they were marvellous. And they love that. My father was no different.'

Her brothers found their father intimidating, though Appelbaum insists that she never did: 'I'm not easily intimidated by anybody. In fact, I can't think of anybody that I find intimidating.'

It is no surprise that people close to Appelbaum see her – rather than her two older brothers – as a chip off the old block.

'It is not a bad old block to be a chip of. I am definitely the most similar to my father,' she laughs.

When the block appointed the chip as a director of Liberty Investors Ltd, the group's holding company, he didn't expect to hear a peep out of her. Wrong. The feisty Appelbaum had no intention of sitting and nodding through meetings. In her first Liberty meeting, she piped up with some questions. Her father kept a poker face but, when the meeting was over, he pulled his daughter aside. He told her that he never wanted to hear her question him in the boardroom again.

'I said: "What do you think I'm doing here? If you want a rubber stamp, go to the post office. I'm not here to rubber-stamp anything." Nobody else would take him on. I was always the one who had to do it.'

The one characteristic of her father's that irked Appelbaum the most was, in her own words, that 'He was a sexist.'

Aside from her, Sir Donald never appointed a woman to a management position, Appelbaum says. He also called businesswomen who didn't say much 'very clever'.

'I thought to myself: "Oh no, you have a problem." I never saw him put a woman into an important position, ever. It frustrated me.'

Her father's condescending attitude in the boardroom was an eye-opener, Appelbaum says, which helped forge her into a feminist. Gordon may have taught his daughter to stand up for herself, but it was an activist from the United States who truly lit the way. Women's rights activist Gloria Steinem later became a friend.

'I am not a bra-burning feminist. I associate closely with Gloria because she has been able to maintain her femininity despite her belief in equality. I believe that women are equal to men, if not better. There is nothing, aside from hard physical labour, that women can't do as well as men. Many women just haven't had the opportunities.'

South Africa may have been slow when it comes to the cause of women, but if Letty Impey was alive today, she would have been surprised, to say the least, at Appelbaum's outspoken feminism. In 1894, Impey became the first woman in recorded history who was allowed to work in an office in Johannesburg. She was a secretary for solicitor Henry Lindsay. Her employment caused so much scandal that Impey had to work with screens around her, as it was deemed 'not quite proper' for her to be seen, according to City of Johannesburg records. This caused much peeking by and disruption among the men in the office, who couldn't believe that a woman had been allowed into their enclave.

Perhaps women have moved on in the past century, but not enough, says Appelbaum, who believes the screens around Letty Impey are far from symbolically gone. 'There are some boards who really believe that women should be seen but not heard and who are taken aback when you give them an opinion,' she claims. 'You just have to take a look at some of the companies headed by women in this country and their female representation. You'd be deeply disappointed. Perhaps women don't want to be seen rocking the boat.'

Appelbaum complains about what she calls 'repeat board seats', where a select few women (appointed by men) sit on many boards, fooling the world into thinking women have shattered the glass ceiling.

'If you look at how many women are exposed, it's very low. There's no point in one woman sitting on 10 corporate boards and filling out long forms of conflicts of interest prior to meetings. That's nonsense. Women must get to the point where they widen the spread of individuals exposed at those levels. We're making slow progress in giving women the equal opportunities they so rightly deserve.'

It was this zeal that led Appelbaum to one of her crowning moments as a start-up entrepreneur. It was the uncertain, yet hopeful, days of 1994 in South Africa. Apartheid was over and democracy was taking its first, wobbly steps. The ANC had taken over the political kingdom and was seeking to help black entrepreneurs scale the heights of white business.

'It was Valhalla for black empowerment deals in those days,' one veteran Johannesburg-based black financial analyst recalls fondly. 'You could go into a business with a consortium, tell the owners why they needed a black-owned stake in the company and walk out with a deal.'

As black businesswomen looked on, they realised that it was the men who were getting the most out of the new dispensation. They had an epiphany at a workshop aimed at informing black business of the new opportunities opening up.

'That workshop was full of men,' says entrepreneur Louisa Mojela, one of the few women who attended it. In the wake of the workshop, Mojela, Wendy Luhabe, Gloria Serobe and Nomhle Canca met every week in Luhabe's tiny office in Melville, Johannesburg. All four were in business, and over a period of 18 months and numerous cups of tea, they sketched out a plan to bring more women into the fold.

'We underestimated the task until we were in it,' says Serobe. 'There was a big mountain to climb. Whether it was about chauvinist or racist men, we knew this was the world we were getting into and we had to find a way to adapt.'

They thought of the women with whom they had grown up in the small towns of South Africa – tough women who worked their fingers to the bone just so that they could set aside a little money every month. The four businesswomen came up with the idea to give these women the opportunity to invest in some of South Africa's biggest companies, such as Old Mutual and Nedbank.

This was the foundation of Women Investment Portfolio Holdings (Wiphold), a company that would turn an initial $60 000 investment into a $120-million, debt-free enterprise listed on the JSE. Wiphold is 55 per cent black-owned, with a female board and 250 000 indirect women beneficiaries – those from the small towns.

The founders invited Wendy Appelbaum, with her considerable business experience and boardroom muscle, into the fledgling company.

'We were 11 women on the board,' recalls Appelbaum. 'The timing was perfect. BEE was becoming the sexy thing of the day. And when you coupled that with women ... the deal flow was extraordinary.'

The management team went out among the women of the towns and villages with programmes to tutor them in basic finance, and helped them form groups to pool money to invest. Appelbaum threw her energy into problem-solving and opening up new investment opportunities.

'Failure did not exist in her books,' recalls Mojela two decades later. 'Beneath that toughness there is an element of softness, kindness and a huge heart to give to the previously disadvantaged. She treats her colleagues with a lot of respect and humility.'

Appelbaum left Wiphold shortly after it listed, selling her shares so that previously disadvantaged women could benefit. 'I thought there was enough strength in the company to continue without me. Although white women also fell into the previously disadvantaged group at that time, I certainly didn't feel it myself. I didn't think I should benefit,' she says.

'It was probably one of the most effective boards I have ever sat on. There is no bullshit with women. We don't waste time out of politeness ... Women have intuition, which men don't have, and [there is] probably a softer side to us, on a certain level, where compassion does come in. It gives you a much more interesting and varied vision of the world. Men see the big picture; women see detail. And it is when the two work together that you get a much better outcome for the business.'

From boardroom grit to grapes two decades later – one of Appelbaum's greatest challenges as an entrepreneur came late in life, when she went into the wine business.

Her decision to purchase a wine farm drew knowing smiles among wealthy South Africans. After all, an old joke that still does the rounds at the top business tables is: How do you make a small fortune? Take a big fortune and invest it in the wine business.

And the wine industry, a highly competitive, low-margin business, *is* a hard nut to crack. One of the industry's most enduring questions is: How do so many players manage to get so much wine into so many bottles so cheaply *and still make a profit*? The short answer? Most of them don't.

Appelbaum, however, approached the industry with much enthusiasm. Her aim was to produce top-quality organic wine. She acquired DeMorgenzon – the morning sun – with her husband Hylton. The wine estate is situated in the hills of the Stellenbosch winelands about 45 minutes' drive from Cape Town. Appelbaum has also made the estate her home. She lives in a manor house on the higher ground of the estate, from where she can look down on her vineyards. The first vintage from this estate, a 2005 Chenin Blanc, earned five stars in South Africa's *Platter's Wine Guide*.

'I am an absolute perfectionist,' she admits. 'Whatever I decide to do, I will drive myself insane until it is done right.'

Her competitive streak, nurtured as a child, drives her in life and in business. She was a provincial tennis player as a child and a provincial golfer later in life.

'It's my way or the highway. But only because I am so sure of what I want.'

Appelbaum poured her canny, disciplined nature and business experience into her vineyards. In the cause of organic wine, she planted wildflowers between the vines for natural pollination and played baroque music to the grapes from loudspeakers to help them grow.

'Professor Lise Korsten from the University of Pretoria was very interested in what we were doing. She was involved in sound-wave study and its effects on plants and insects. Some preliminary trials were done on playing our baroque music to fungi in petri dishes under controlled conditions. Early indications were that the fungi growing with baroque music showed a more even and upright growing pattern.

'We have also been approached by scientists involved in agricultural telepathy, the field where they study how plants, animals and humans communicate. One particular Dutch scientist showed us some fascinating studies of how plants communicate by linking up a plant to a digital synthesiser and playing the frequencies through speakers.'

It is only the weather Appelbaum can't orchestrate, and it is one of the factors of the wine industry that concerns her.

'For a control freak like me, the wine business is a hell of a challenge. It's very frustrating. Farmers who did not have supplementary irrigation and who farmed in low rainfall areas, such as Darling and the Swartland, suffered massive losses in 2016; up to 50 per cent losses in certain areas. Stellenbosch farms, which have a greater maritime influence and higher annual rainfall, suffered less, although the drought resulted in an earlier and smaller harvest.

'The trend over the last few years has been earlier harvest and less rainfall in the months of January and February. Winter rainfall over the last few years has also been lower than normal, with most dams not filling to capacity. More reservoirs will need to be built, and the industry will naturally start considering grape varieties that do better in drought conditions, such as Grenache Blanc and Grenache noir, and there will be a shift to wine styles that rely less on longer hang times, i.e. longer time of the fruit hanging on the vine, thereby limiting the water requirement of the vineyard.

'Fruit will be picked earlier, producing lighter, fresher styles of wines. Government is becoming increasingly vigilant in monitoring all water uses on farms, and the long-term result may be increased taxes on vineyards that are heavily reliant on supplementary irrigation.'

Appelbaum's dream of becoming a wine exporter is equally complex.

'We have had limited success in Zimbabwe, and a few small outlets in Namibia. It has not been a major focus of ours, with our local market and key export markets growing more rapidly. Small amounts of wine have been shipped to Nigeria. Import legislation in Nigeria is definitely a barrier to entry, with onerous control measures being placed on all importers, which lead to very lengthy and expensive processes before a product can be imported,' she explains.

Appelbaum took her time finding the right winemaker. Many have been called but few are chosen for DeMorgenzon. 'I had four or five winemakers making wine for me. Not only did I look at the quality of the wine they made, but for a number of years I interacted with them to see with whom I would get on best. The winemaker is the one who grows grapes to their best advantage. What I have to do as the entrepreneur is to give him every opportunity to grow the best wine he can.'

The staff at DeMorgenzon appear to appreciate Appelbaum's no-nonsense approach. Diana Renke, the tasting-room manager at the time, said, 'What you see is what you get. She has a very transparent management style. She tells you things straight.'

The wine business led Appelbaum into a dust-up that was to test her integrity in the full glare of publicity, which she has spent most of her life avoiding. It all began in December 2011, when she bid $6.5 million for her second wine estate, Quoin Rock Wine Estate and Manor House. On that day she smelt a rat with the auction process and decided to take on the multimillion-dollar auctioneering industry in order to protect her own integrity.

Appelbaum laid a complaint with the National Consumer Commission (NCC) in which she claimed that she had competed against a ghost bidder for the estate. She claimed that South Africa's largest auction group, Auction Alliance, had hired this ghost bidder to drive up the price. It turned into a very public spat with Auction Alliance CEO Rael Levitt.

'Mr Levitt took me out of my comfort zone,' Appelbaum says, 'because he chose to fight me in the media. That fight with Mr Levitt was a fight for good. For me, there's either right or wrong. There's nothing grey in this matter. I believe that I have done South African society a great service, because corruption is rife in this country.'

The outcome proved her right. The NCC found Auction Alliance guilty of contravening the Consumer Protection Act by conducting what it saw as a 'mock auction' and fined it 10 per cent of its annual turnover.

Appelbaum's love of a good fight stems in part from her friendship with Helen Suzman, the staunch anti-apartheid activist and a family friend of the Gordons. Suzman was also the daughter of Lithuanian immigrants.

'She was a no-bullshit woman – tough, clever and not intimidated by anybody. She encouraged me to be feisty and cheeky. She would fight anybody as long as it was for somebody's benefit,' Appelbaum recalls.

One of Appelbaum's few regrets is that she never became a doctor, a profession of which her father, who wanted her to be an accountant like him, disapproved. In spite of raising several objections, she was thwarted by the sexist selection processes of the time. In those years, people were not only held back by race restrictions, but also strict gender quotas. Appelbaum was a woman.

Instead of pursuing her dream, she studied psychology and economics. But her desire to do something in medicine never left her, and a lifetime later a large chunk of her philanthropic work focuses on health. She is a trustee of the Donald Gordon Foundation, established by her father, one of the largest private charitable foundations in southern Africa. The foundation oversees the running of the Donald Gordon Medical Centre in Johannesburg, as well as the Wendy Appelbaum Institute for Women's Health.

Appelbaum is also a trustee of CHOC Children's, which focuses on haematology and oncology research for children's diseases, and she has enrolled at Harvard Medical School to study the connection between human rights and healthcare.

Armed with fresh knowledge, you can be sure Appelbaum will be up for any fight. Heaven help anyone who stands in her way.

15

Court battles and 'no' to corruption – a Tour de Strive

Strive Masiyiwa

Strive Masiyiwa

I N MY DARKER hours, I think of an inspiring day in Nairobi that rarely fails to lift the gloom.

It was the day I met Anindo Murunga, a 14-year-old boarder at Kenya High School in Nairobi. Anindo was a youngster with a mind as sharp as a scalpel. In many ways, she embodied the spirit I hoped to capture with *Forbes Africa* – that it would not merely be a business magazine, but a journal to educate and inspire; to arm a rising generation of Africans with the tools to build their continent.

A year earlier, Anindo's mother Christine, who was now sitting with her daughter across the table from me in a Nairobi hotel, wrote this to me:

I have decided to write and thank you for the influence you have been having on my daughter with your articles. My daughter is aged 13 years and has been begging the uncle to share his old Forbes magazines for her reading. I got curious because despite buying other types of magazines she hasn't shown interest in my selection. When she requested I get her a copy of her own magazine I said it was too costly of which she answered 'please mum, get Ksh. 500/-only from my pocket money and assign me extra duties so that you can buy me the magazine.' Of which I responded I would, then, she quickly pointed out; 'buy FORBES AFRICA!'

Anindo appeared well acquainted with the prevailing opinions on business in Africa. 'I like the way [Aliko] Dangote has diversified his business across the continent so that he has reduced the risk of collapse,' she told me.

She said she wanted to study automotive mechanical engineering in

Germany where, she told me, the schools are the best in the field. She planned to return to Nairobi to start her own business after her 25th birthday. She had just joined an investment club at school.

'Recently I won 5,000ksh in a value-investment challenge. With this money I plan to buy 100 shares from Safaricom company. Later this year, I will participate in a competition whereby a team of five comes up with a business plan that will be developed into a company if the team wins.

'I love to read about how entrepreneurs struggled to make it. We can learn from them and we can also make it.'

I asked Anindo whether she wanted to be on the cover of *Forbes Africa*. She thought deeply for a while. 'In 2035,' she said with quiet confidence.

Anindo has read about scores of billionaires and millionaires in *Forbes Africa*, but there is no doubt which one is her hero: the battle-scarred telecommunications multimillionaire Strive Masiyiwa of Zimbabwe.

'His stand against corruption made me admire him,' says Anindo.

Masiyiwa had defied bullying authorities in his own backyard to build a billion-dollar empire across 17 countries, from Latin America to Europe and the Pacific. In many ways, he is the authentic African entrepreneur, one that people look up to in the 21st century. A quiet, modest man who prefers to stay out of the limelight, the big names nevertheless beat a path to his door. The then Senator Barack Obama had lunch with Masiyiwa in Johannesburg in 2006. When Obama became head of the Free World, he invited Masiyiwa to the White House to speak on global development. Masiyiwa was probably as star-struck as anyone when he revealed the following on his Facebook page:

During our lunch, I quickly recognized Senator Obama as a man of great vision – a leader with a heart not just for the people in his own country, but for the whole world, and for the African continent in particular. He did not need me to tell him that women smallholder farmers are the backbone for agriculture in the developing world, or that in parts of Africa and India, close to 40% of children are stunted, or that over one billion people still have no access to electricity. He already knew.

There is no doubt that Masiyiwa is a devout, principled man. At one stage in his life, he wanted to become a guerrilla fighter, but instead he ended up fighting a bruising court battle against the government for which he had once contemplated taking up arms. Masiyiwa is a frontrunner in fibre optics and operates the continent's largest satellite communications business. Add fixed and enterprise networks and you have Econet Wireless — one of the largest telecommunications companies in the world.

In 2015, Econet had 30 million mobile customers, thousands of corporate clients and almost 6 000 employees. The company generated an estimated $3 billion in annual revenue, which was probably a conservative figure.

There is no doubt that Masiyiwa has written entrepreneurial history in Africa. His Econet group has thrived on constant reinvention and an aggressive expansion into new countries. According to *Forbes*, it has earned him a fortune of $600 million.

A former business associate says, 'He has a dictatorial streak in him that knows no bounds. I suppose in business, it's a dog-eat-dog world, but Strive can push you to the limits. He knows what he wants and, if an opportunity arises, you can wholeheartedly bank on him.'

Twenty years ago, less than 1 per cent of Africans had a telephone. Today, Africa is the talking continent, with three out of four Africans owning a cellphone. It's one of the most shining successes in the history of business on the continent.

'There are more cellphones in Africa today than in Europe,' Masiyiwa claims. 'More Africans have access to the internet via the cellphone than Europeans. There's a tsunami of data. People talk less on their cellphones than they use data. The traditional cellphone networks can't carry that. You just have to look post-voice.'

Econet's British subsidiary, Liquid Telecom, now runs Africa's longest network across 14 borders, from Cape Town via Kigali, Kampala and Nairobi, all the way up to Mogadishu. Its fibre-optics customers are mainly large corporations, including mining and oil companies, internet service and mobile providers, and banks.

In 2016, Liquid Telecom was on the acquisition trail. The unlisted pan-African group, majority owned by Econet Global, bought South African telecoms company Neotel for $428 million. The deal, subject to regulatory approval, will make Liquid Telecom the largest pan-African broadband network, spanning 12 countries, with 40 000 kilometres of cross-border, metro and access-fibre networks, the group said in a statement.

Christopher Mugaga, the head of research at Econometer Global Capital, says: '[Masiyiwa] is a principled business tycoon who managed to look beyond the dynamics of Harare, especially from the economic and political facets, to go into business, which brought him to the fore as one of the world's most recognisable personalities. He refused to be associated with corrupt practices in today's Africa.'

The deal will also give Liquid Telecom a better grip on the South African market. It already operates in Botswana, the Democratic Republic of Congo, Kenya, Lesotho, Rwanda, Uganda, Zambia and Zimbabwe.

'They are plugging in a very big gap that exists in Africa,' says Johannesburg-based TechCentral editor Duncan McLeod. 'Masiyiwa is a shrewd operator who is very connected, and he understands the market as well as the conditions on the ground. He knows how to operate in tough business environments and how to make the best of it.'

This tale of acquisition and expansion must have seemed a universe away when Masiyiwa sat in a musty courtroom in Harare in the 1990s, looking over at the dour faces of the government officials and their lawyers who were intent upon strangling his business at birth.

By this time Masiyiwa had already made his mark as an entrepreneur in Zimbabwe's post-independence boom period after he'd returned from years in exile. The Masiyiwa family had fled the then Rhodesia in 1965 after Ian Smith's Unilateral Declaration of Independence in November of that year, which entrenched white minority rule and cemented Rhodesia's place as an international pariah, leading to crippling sanctions.

It was in exile in Zambia that Masiyiwa had his first glimpse of what it takes to become a successful entrepreneur. His mother founded a furniture business in Kitwe, in Zambia's then booming copper belt, which was soon thriving.

From the age of seven, Strive, his brother and his sister helped out in the workshop, which helped pay for their education at a private boarding school in Edinburgh, Scotland.

'My mother manufactured and sold her own furniture. She was very good at it. It was a typical African family business. You are part and parcel of what goes on in it. I learnt a lot of the basics from her, including the importance of hard work,' Masiyiwa recalls. 'The most important aspect of a business is its people; how you motivate them, how you keep them. Those are enduring principles.'

Even though Masiyiwa had left his home country at a young age, he always longed to return to Zimbabwe. When he finished school, he planned to join the guerrillas in the armed struggle against Smith's ruling white minority. But then he realised that an education might be a better weapon with which to fight injustice. He studied electrical and electronic engineering in the UK, then returned to Zimbabwe in 1984 to work for the national telephone company ZPTC.

The sleepy government-run telephone company had a monopoly at the time, and was regularly derided by the population for running a poor network. It often took more than 20 attempts to dial a number just around the corner. ZPTC also struggled to connect a growing new black middle class. Its slow-moving gangs of workers excavating by the roadside earned ZPTC the derisive nickname in chiShona, *Pasi Tino Chera* (down with those who dig trenches).

It is no surprise that the dynamic young Masiyiwa didn't stay at ZPTC for long.

'I decided that it really wasn't for me to work for an enterprise, so I started my own business. Because there were no opportunities in telecommunications, I changed sectors and started a construction firm,' Masiyiwa says.

It was the right move at the right time. Retrofit, his construction business, snapped up lucrative government and private-sector contracts throughout Zimbabwe.

'Even if you visit Harare today, there is hardly a major building that I wasn't involved in,' says Masiyiwa.

Even in the good years, Masiyiwa never forgot his training as a telecommunications engineer, and in the early 1990s talk turned to the boundless possibilities in his former field.

'As soon as I saw that the telecommunications sector was opening up, I began to pursue that,' he recalls. He had powerful foreign investors, but it wasn't that simple. Up until then, the state-controlled ZPTC had clung doggedly to its monopoly, but now government was about to grant more licences, making the industry more competitive. The government also wanted to open up its own mobile-phone network, but it was far from ready, even though it had flown in equipment to set it up.

When Masiyiwa, then in his 30s, approached his former employer in 1993 with plans for a wireless joint venture, ZPTC said no. They distrusted the bright young man who had beaten the state into setting up an independent mobile network in what everyone knew could be a booming business.

'This boy has beaten you,' President Robert Mugabe allegedly told his cabinet, and instructed them to stop Masiyiwa.

In order to take on the government, Masiyiwa needed all the business acumen, determination, aggression and faith he had at his disposal. At that time, cellphones were virtually non-existent, and Masiyiwa wanted to lead the way. Instead, the government awarded licences to state-owned companies NetOne and Telecel, giving them a head start in the market. NetOne was seen as a standard-bearer for the government; ministers used to hand out NetOne SIM cards at party meetings.

'Ah, you are still supporting us!' presidential spokesman George Charamba once said to a journalist colleague of mine after she had called him on a NetOne phone.

But Masiyiwa was not about to give up. Instead, he came up with Plan B, which had originated from a surprising source. Masiyiwa revealed on his Facebook page that it was former cabinet minister Edson Zvobgo who had tipped him off that the right to open communication was entrenched as 'a beacon of freedom' in Clause 20 of the constitution of Zimbabwe. Negotiated at the Lancaster House talks that had helped create Zimbabwe in 1979, the clause reads: 'Every Zimbabwean shall have the right to impart information without hindrance.'

Zvobgo was one of the politicians who had negotiated the agreement. In his obituary in 2004, the *Standard* in Harare wrote: 'Ten days before the signing of the Lancaster House Agreement, he raised temperatures on a cold day in England by telling Margaret Thatcher to "jump into the Thames".'

As if this was not enough, Zvobgo went on to insinuate that Thatcher was having an affair with 'Satan Botha'. PW Botha was the South African prime minister at the time. When Zvobgo felt that Lord Carrington, who was chairing the Lancaster peace talks, was trying to extract too many concessions from the Patriotic Front without corresponding pressure being applied on Ian Smith and Abel Muzorewa, he lashed out: 'If Carrington carries on the way he has begun, plotting with puppets, we will go back to war.'

More than a quarter of a century later, Clause 20 of the Lancaster House–negotiated constitution would prove manna from heaven for Strive Masiyiwa.

'Being able to talk to someone on a telephone is part of freedom of expression, I thought. That means that monopolies restrict freedom of expression.'

It led to a bruising court battle that took years to conclude and brought Masiyiwa international publicity. It also made him rather unpopular with his government. Even the media who reported on the story became unpopular with the people in power. One of them was the well-known, award-winning reporter Barnabas Thondhlana, a true character of journalism. Dedicated to his craft but with a twinkle in his eye and a smile rarely far from his lips, Thondhlana soon discovered that the Strive Masiyiwa story was no laughing matter.

More than 20 years later, he recalls: 'Threats came thick and fast from government, but my editor, Trevor Ncube, was not moved by the threats and encouraged us to continue running the story, firstly in the *Financial Gazette* and then the *Zimbabwe Independent*, which we launched in 1996. I was awarded the News Reporter of the Year Award at the National Journalists Awards in 1995 for the exposé.

'We were sued for running the stories, of course. We had the necessary documents to prove our case, but what worked in our favour in one of the cases was that the then [Z]PTC company secretary, who had just been fired – and was disgruntled – came to fight in our corner in court. And he came with suitcases full of documents from his days at the [Z]PTC.'

The furore spelt the end of Masiyiwa's construction business. As soon as he took on the government, doors slammed in his face.

'The day we filed the case, every single contract we had with any government organisation ended,' he says.

He, his wife and six children were also constantly harassed by the police and intelligence officers.

Thondhlana recalls that politicians were clearly rattled by the case.

'At some later stage I was approached by another cabinet minister, who warned me that I should go easy on linking the government minister to the saga, as, in his own words: "The corridors where my name was being mentioned were not good and could result in my disappearance." I took the warning and went easy on him! Together with other journalists who were also running the Econet story, we were labelled "Strive's Boys"!'

Meanwhile, Masiyiwa was struggling to sell his construction business.

'I scrambled to sell the business because we were taking on the government in court in Retrofit's name. When I eventually found a buyer, he said I needed to resolve the dispute first. But I couldn't wait years, so I set up a new company, Econet, and transferred the litigation to the new company,' he explains.

It was a very tough time, but his faith kept him going. The court battle coincided with a spiritual awakening, Masiyiwa says, even though he had grown up in a family not too concerned with religion.

'When I was in my mid-30s, I came across the Bible and made a commitment to become a Christian and live life according to certain values,' he says. 'When you have faith, you don't see obstacles. Knowing God was on my side, I never had a sense of struggle.'

Masiyiwa became a born-again Christian, and that sustained him through his financial and legal troubles.

'In fact, it was the church that carried me through. They rallied behind me in an extraordinary way,' he says.

Many Zimbabweans supported Masiyiwa's case against the government. As economic conditions deteriorated in the country, the people on the ground were forgetting the loyalties that were forged in the fervour of liberation in favour of holding the people in power accountable. Despite the turbulent times, people would walk up to Masiyiwa in the street to offer their hand in solidarity. Some promised not to buy a cellphone until Masiyiwa was allowed to operate in the country.

It took years before the case was finally concluded, on 30 December 1997. Masiyiwa recalls that day on his Facebook page:

The night of 30th December 1997, in Boston, will forever be one of the most incredible spiritual experiences of my life. As I slept, I had a dream, and in it I saw a judge sitting down to read a ruling. It was so vivid, and one thing I distinctly remembered was that the judge was white, and all our lawyers were there, as were the lawyers of the company that had been awarded the tender. The judge was very angry, and declared that the courts were upset that this case kept coming back to them. He then declared Econet licensed, and said [his verdict] would never be overturned. I woke up to find that it was about 2am. To be honest with you, I do not really care much for dreams, even today, and I always caution on taking dreams seriously, unless you have really prayed.

After some time of prayer, I called my colleague Zac Wazara in Harare, on the hotel phone. I asked him to enquire of our lawyers if there had been any developments. He called back a few minutes later to say that Tawanda Nyambirai had told him that the courts were closed for the holidays, until mid-January.

After Zac's call, I got dressed and then began to pray again, as I was now unable to sleep; about 30 mins or so later, the phone rang. It was Zac Wazara: 'Justice Sandura's clerk has just summoned all the lawyers to court. Apparently, he has been promoted to the Supreme Court, from the High Court. He has been working during the holiday to clear his High Court cases. He is about to hand down the ruling!'

Justice Sandura overturned the award of the licence to the other companies, and declared us, 'duly licensed'. It was an emphatic court victory.

Masiyiwa wasted no time getting the company off the ground, and Econet shot to market leader within six weeks of being licensed. It made Masiyiwa a multimillionaire.

'It must have been a Holy War for him,' says Thondhlana. 'He [Strive] believes firmly in God, and his faith pulled him through. It was a very difficult period for him. Aftermath: The Strive story killed whatever hopes some of us had of launching ourselves into business. Despite launching our own newspapers, they collapsed due to the lack of advertising from the biggest advertiser – government – as we had been blacklisted. And in any case, even the Econet adverts never came! But looking back, I am glad my stories made a difference.'

Masiyiwa never forgot the support his fellow churchgoers lent him in those rough times. Every year, he donates a sizeable chunk of his income to his church. He also listed Econet's Zimbabwean subsidiary partially on the Harare Stock Exchange. Econet, otherwise, remains a private business.

'When I got my licence, I felt I had to give those who supported me an opportunity to be owners in my company. I wanted them to be more than just customers. So I sold 40 per cent of the subsidiary and kept the rest. I decided it was the best way to show my appreciation,' he says.

'The response was phenomenal. We have the largest and widest owner-ship of any company in Zimbabwe.'

Not only Zimbabweans, but people across the continent can be grateful to Masiyiwa, as the court case opened up Africa's telecommunications sector to private capital, making mobile phones affordable and ubiquitous. Many more have since made their fortune through the freedom of the airwaves and people's insatiable desire to communicate.

Econet was also Masiyiwa's stepping stone to creating an Africa-centred, global corporation. He launched Econet all over the continent and moved the company to South Africa in 2000. Today he shuttles between Econet's headquarters in Johannesburg and London, where his family lives.

Masiyiwa does business on the continent with the same zeal with which he fought his court case. When he set his sights on Kenya, where the government had put the national telephone company up for tender, he was awarded the tender but declined to take up the deal.

'The people who were in office had strange ideas about how to do business,' he explains. 'After a very inappropriate proposal came through, I said, "Thank you, but no thank you," and called off the deal.'

It prompted Masiyiwa's fervent crusade against corruption. He subsequently abandoned a handful of lucrative but non-transparent government tenders in Nigeria, Malawi and Cameroon.

'Dealing with corruption is simple. You walk away,' he says, claiming he has never paid a bribe and simply says no when they are suggested. 'It's not the end of the world if the deal doesn't happen. I have no regrets.'

He admits, however, that he has been persecuted for his tough stance against corruption. At times he has had to wait years to launch operations in a country because of corrupt officials blocking the way.

In Kenya, his resolve and patience eventually paid off. A couple of years after he'd walked away from the telephone tender, Kenya's leadership was replaced in general elections.

'The new government called me and asked me to bid for another licence, promising me [that the process] was going to be open and transparent. I bid and won that tender, and began to build a new business in Kenya, which I subsequently sold to [French mobile provider] Orange,' Masiyiwa says.

Instead of wasting his energy on dubious deals, Masiyiwa focuses on staying on top of his game in Africa. He is a visionary who must not be underestimated, says Arthur Goldstuck, director of business-technology research firm World Wide Worx in Johannesburg.

'He created a real pan-African business in a sector dominated by foreign firms and foreign investment. What makes Masiyiwa unique is his pan-African approach, while also branching out elsewhere in the world. He doesn't see Africa as a limitation. That's very rare.'

The next big thing for Masiyiwa is the small screen. In June 2016 he announced the launch of Kwesé TV – a word in chiShona that means 'everywhere' – in 44 countries across Africa. Fledgling media organisations have been the graveyard of many a good entrepreneur, but Masiyiwa seems to think he is on to a winner. He started by employing 80 people, and by the end of 2016 had plans to increase the payroll to 2000.

'I will not launch a business where there are existing competitors unless I can identify at least five "insights"; you might call them "game-changers". I must then hold these insights close to my chest, like a good chess player. If the game intensifies, I must be able to generate at least five more in "quick fire"! Finding the "insights" requires hours and hours of continued study and research into an industry. This type of study is like an immersion – you must eat, sleep, think, think, think, learn, learn!' Masiyiwa said in a statement at the launch.

Masiyiwa commits considerable time outside of business to charities and trusts, including the Rockefeller Foundation, AGRA, which represents smallholder farmers, the United Nations' panel for sustainable energy, and Kofi Annan's Africa Progress Panel. Bill Clinton appointed Masiyiwa to the board of the Southern Africa Enterprise Development Fund, and he also sits on the boards of the Nelson Mandela Advisory Committee and Endeavor South Africa.

Morehouse College, one of the most respected universities in the United States – civil rights leader Martin Luther King Jr was an alumni – honoured Masiyiwa's humanitarian work and philanthropy with an honorary doctorate.

Closer to home, he financially supports 42 000 orphans in South Africa, Zimbabwe, Lesotho and Burundi through the Capernaum Trust, which he established with his wife Tsitsi.

Together with British entrepreneur Richard Branson, Masiyiwa runs the Carbon War Room, an international non-profit organisation that helps entrepreneurs develop solutions to fight climate change.

'Strive is passionate about Africa gaining full economic freedom,' Branson wrote in his latest book, *Screw Business As Usual*. He also credited Masiyiwa as one of the people who brought about the communications revolution. No wonder Masiyiwa is often referred to as the Bill Gates of Africa – a backhanded compliment he takes in his stride.

'I thought Bill was the Strive Masiyiwa of America!' he quips.

16

Right place, wrong business, right time

Patrice Motsepe

Patrice Motsepe

M Y FIRST MEETING with Patrice Motsepe occurred at the most frantic moment, at the birth of *Forbes Africa*. For me, it was indeed the best of times and the worst of times.

Hectic activity had gobbled up the weeks leading up to the launch of *Forbes Africa* like a hungry beast. There were numerous boardroom meetings, late nights poring over stories, appearances on radio and television to punt the launch, and endless hours appointing freelancers and working out how to pay them in various countries across Africa.

The first cover – the most historic and important part of the first issue – was pushed to the back of our minds in these dizzy days. After all, it was going to be as easy as shelling peas to get someone to accept the honour of being on the first cover, wasn't it?

The cover story is the magazine's banner; it is our pride and joy and our shop window. I believe that the dramatic yet simple appeal of an influential and successful face, coupled with a fascinating background story, is a magnet to the human eye. It can also give the editor a lifetime supply of headaches.

When I network at functions, people often say how exciting it must be to talk to the most powerful men and women on the continent. It is, but to get billionaires and multimillionaires on the cover, you have to have buckets full of patience … and aspirin.

For the cover is the page that inspires the most passion, arguments and anger; it is the page that readers are the quickest to judge. You may have won a Pulitzer Prize with one of your stories inside the magazine, but the cover will always hog the limelight.

'One thing I respect about *Forbes Africa* is that you don't put just anyone on the front,' Zoli Kunene, a veteran South African lawyer and businessman, told me at a company function.

Many magazines struggle with their cover. They run through all the obvious people, then start putting just about anyone they can find on the front. Up pop ten-a-penny DJs, CEOs and motivational speakers; down goes the credibility of the magazine.

Remember, your readers are your harshest critics. I always tell my young journalists that our readers are the ones who spend their money, so they have every right to be critical. If every business remembered that the customer is always right, there would be more successful businesses.

People ask why we put only rich people on the cover. Well, hello, we are a magazine concerned with the business of entrepreneurs and how they made their money. Why don't we put sportsmen on the front? We are not a sports magazine. The list goes on – DJs, musicians, scientists ... We are a *business* magazine.

Needless to say, 99 per cent of those who ask these questions will be the first ones to cry, 'Who the heck is this?' if we ever did break the mould.

For the first edition of *Forbes Africa*, the idea was to make a splash – the bigger the better. We wanted the two best-known names in business on the African continent: the Nigerian cement billionaire Aliko Dangote, and South African mining billionaire Patrice Motsepe. Motsepe was worth $1.6 billion, making him the 15th-richest man in Africa (according to the *Forbes* 2017 list).

We toyed with the idea to get Dangote and Motsepe standing back to back on the first cover under the headline 'The Big Fight'. The article would examine the two billionaires' fascinating stories, offset against a report on the competition between the mighty economies of South Africa and Nigeria. It was a good idea, as well as ambitious. The only problem was that we needed to get two very busy tycoons to two cover shoots – with lights and backdrops, the lot – at either end of the continent. It was a mammoth task even on a good day.

The bigger problem was that we couldn't raise either of them for love or money. Every day I rang the Lagos office, which claimed close contact with Dangote's people, all in vain. In Johannesburg, we put our faith in Vuyo Mvoko, a respected, well-connected South African political journalist and one of our first freelancers, who was trying to get us to Motsepe. After all, Motsepe was a solid-gold bet for a magazine intent on telling the African story – the son of a chief who became a lawyer and struck a blow for black business by taking on the white-dominated mining industry at its own game.

In 2008, our colleagues at *Forbes* in New York had created a stir by putting Motsepe on their cover, calling him the first black South African billionaire. Everyone in Africa knew Motsepe, from taxi drivers to senior civil servants.

The days ticked by, and nothing happened. We gave up on Dangote for sheer lack of time. In hindsight, it was a move that proved a blessing in disguise. It paid off months later, when Dangote agreed to a stunning cover.

To get hold of Motsepe, we had tried official letters and telephone entreaties. It was getting serious – we were left with days before the deadline for the picture, as well as a compelling 3 000-word cover story, of which we had not so much as a comma. It was a deeply worrying time – I put on a brave face. Our boss, vice-chairman Rakesh Wahi, who had spent a lifetime starting up businesses, warned us that one could never launch anything without getting a bloody nose. Imagine us bleeding at the first step? It didn't bear thinking about.

We kept on writing letters and making calls. I had worked with Vuyo for many years and I leant on him to help us out of the crisis. One of the sticking points was that Motsepe's people wanted our assurance that he would be on the cover. This is an assurance we never give, even in a crisis such as this one.

Then, even worse, Motsepe's office wanted to read the story before publication. This went against every journalistic ethic, as well as the strict rules set by *Forbes* in the United States. I assured Motsepe's people that we always double-checked all the facts before we published and stuck to my guns. I reiterated that they would not see the copy before publication, much to their chagrin. They muttered that the man himself was a lawyer who was familiar with libel laws and informed me that the richest man in South Africa would ring me to discuss the matter further. I said a silent prayer and steeled myself for the phone call.

'Let's put this behind us and move forward,' Motsepe told me an hour later. I punched the air. Then, as I put the phone down, I leapt up and punched the air again. At last, at long last, we had a cover that would sell our debut magazine and prove to Africa that we were serious. Oh, the power of silent prayer.

Vuyo's interview and the photo shoot were arranged for a sunny spring day in September at Motsepe's mansion in Bryanston, in the plush northern Johannesburg suburbs, where he lives amid vigilant security. As the security men waved us through the gates, it reminded me of my visits to various state houses of Africa. The grounds were vast and scented with blooming spring flowers, and the lawns spread out like lush green carpets. This vision of opulence was surely a good omen for a fledgling magazine about business and wealth.

Motsepe's people had insisted that I be there, as the magazine's editor. I agreed on the grounds that it would be politic to do so and also to ensure, at first hand and for my own sanity, that the shoot was going to go ahead.

We were shown along the lengthy driveway to the Motsepe residence in the blinding spring sunshine. What would we do if the big man cancelled? My heart was in my mouth, even though I didn't let it show to my team.

Finally, we sat down in Motsepe's book-lined study, which overlooks the verdant garden at the back of the house. There is always a bit of trepidation when you are about to meet a powerful man. Motsepe has loads of mystique, as he tends to keep out of the public eye.

We needn't have worried. Motsepe greeted us hale and hearty. The first thing that struck me about him was how affable and personable he was, even giving me a fraternal tap on the arm when emphasising a point. He regaled us with tales of his father's shops near Klerksdorp, in the mining province of North West, where he helped out from the age of six, learning how to grow a business at his father's knee.

'My father taught me a good lesson at a young age. Whenever he made money, he always ploughed it back into the business.'

He told me how he counted the chickens and served behind the counter in the holidays when mineworkers came home in droves to spend their Christmas bonuses.

'You know which entrepreneurs I respect?' Motsepe asked me with a smile. I nodded in expectation. 'Indians,' Motsepe said.

He then told me a story of how he had realised what the essence of an entrepreneur was when their shop had run out of cigarettes early one festive morning.

'We could phone [our Indian suppliers] at three o'clock in the morning, and they would get out of bed, unlock their shop and hand us the cigarettes and say we could pay them tomorrow.'

Motsepe's father, Augustine Butana Chaane Motsepe, who died in 2007 at the age of 92, was the chief of the Bakgatla ba Mmakau tribe. The solid backbone of his family, he was also an ardent critic of the apartheid regime. The flamboyant entrepreneur – family and close friends called him ABC – led his people in a lawsuit against a Canadian company, Leuka Minerals, to claim royalties for the vanadium it was mining on tribal land.

The apartheid authorities didn't take too kindly to the outspoken chief and banished him from Soweto, where Patrice was born, to the family village of Mmakau, north-west of the capital, Pretoria. Motsepe Snr thus became one of generations of enterprising black South Africans who were kept out of mainstream business by apartheid laws. But he would make his mark against the odds. Motsepe Snr opened a grocery store, a beer hall, restaurants and several shopping centres around Mmakau.

'A lot of people do not know that there were very many great black entrepreneurs in the apartheid days,' says Motsepe, who is a prince in his royal Tswana clan. 'We had people like Dr Sam Motsuenyane, Richard Maponya, Habakuk Shikwane ... In many ways, they defied the apartheid laws that restricted them and set up successful businesses. If the playing fields had been level at the time, it would have been so different. It was difficult for those entrepreneurs to even get a general dealer's licence.'

Motsepe learnt to drive, and the young billionaire-to-be delivered crates of beer from his mother's bottle store – the landmark Kay Motsepe Bottle Store – in an old Nissan E20 to the shebeens around Mmakau. Motsepe was also on driving duty, along with his older brother Papi, whenever there was a funeral or wedding, or firewood to be collected. People in Mmakau saw him as a dutiful son.

Motsepe Snr despised apartheid-era Bantu education – where learning was designed to keep people of colour as drawers of water and hewers of wood – and encouraged his children to attend a Catholic mission school so that they could learn and progress. He clearly had ambitions for his son, whom he named after Patrice Lumumba, the first democratically elected president of the Democratic Republic of Congo. Lumumba, who was executed after a short time in office more than half a century ago, is an inspiration to many Africanists across the continent.

'My parents insisted we should always be seen as people who are respectful, never forget where we come from and, more importantly, that we are part of the challenges that face our people. I wouldn't be here today if it wasn't for the way they brought me up.'

Motsepe went on to study at Swaziland University, then attained an LLB at the University of the Witwatersrand in Johannesburg. He became the first black partner at Johannesburg lawyers Bowman Gilfillan, in 1993. Before that, in 1991, he was seconded to work at McGuireWoods in Richmond, Virginia, a measure of the impact he had made at Bowman. It was the kind of career break that could have set Motsepe up very comfortably in life. But he wanted more.

With the advent of democracy in 1994, Motsepe was in the right place at the right time when he decided to venture out on his own as an entrepreneur. South African business and commerce were on the lookout for urbane, bright young boardroom types like Motsepe. Instead, he chose to dip his toe in an unlikely pool – the grimy mining industry, which was old school, white-dominated and almost synonymous with the exploitation that had built the apartheid system.

Even so, the industry has transferred millions of dollars in equity to new black shareholders in the past 20 years, usually in return for deferred dividends, in an attempt to redress the imbalances of the past. This has drawn criticism for creating a crony elite, where the same people are being roped into different boardrooms at the expense of the empty-handed masses.

Motsepe concedes that he benefitted from the new dispensation, but says he did not receive any handouts. Most of his deals were done before the new mining codes, which assisted black people to own a share in the business, were put in place.

'I have never had a government tender,' Motsepe says. 'Of course, if there was no democracy in South Africa, opportunities that opened wouldn't have opened. But if you look at every transaction we did, there was no empowerment.'

True, Motsepe appears to steer clear of politics. Even so, in Africa most billionaires attract attention and agree that it is very difficult to avoid politicians. It is often easier to live and let live.

Motsepe's first entrepreneurial venture, as a contractor on a gold mine, was no indication of the immense success he would later enjoy in business.

'What it entails is going to a mine and asking the bosses what the worst job is on that mine and then ask if you can do it,' he chuckled.

One of the worst jobs on offer then was running sweeping gangs to brush gold dust from the mine workings underground after the mining crews had been through. South Africa's gold mines are deep, hot and water runs everywhere. They are slippery, uncomfortable places to work in, and they get deeper and hotter every year as the quest for gold burrows ever further into the earth.

Motsepe's first contract offered so little income that he couldn't afford to run an office. They called him the 'suitcase man' on the mines, because he ran his small business from a briefcase.

In these lean times, a world away from the luxury of a Johannesburg law firm's spacious offices, Motsepe was wondering how he could improve his business. At a sweeping job in Orkney mine, near Klerksdorp in the North West province, owned by a division of mining giant Anglo American, he offered workers a profit-sharing scheme if they accepted slightly lower wages. It is a deal that is talked about at the mine to this day, not least because Motsepe involved the workers at a time when this was rare. It might not have been a big deal for Motsepe on a financial scale, but it won him a lot of favour. At that point, he also had financial backers behind him for his next move, which was to buy his own mines – the ones no one else wanted.

It wasn't too long before Motsepe was bidding for these mines. He approached Anglo American with an offer to take some of their loss-making, marginal mines off their hands.

'I said: "Go and look at some of your deposits. You will see that some will not suit your long-life, high-grade asset requirements. I can go in there with people who have a history and a track record in small-scale mining."'

It was tough going, even with the support of mining heavyweight Bobby Godsell, the then chief executive of Anglo American's gold and uranium division. In the last days of apartheid, Godsell had been instrumental in connecting South African business leaders with the leadership of the ANC, who would soon assume power in the country. He had always argued passionately for black South Africans who had no capital to get into business. Godsell lobbied the banks to back Motsepe's bid, but they would have none of it. The gold price was in the doldrums and the rand was strengthening, making matters worse.

'Everyone thought I was crazy,' Motsepe recalled about those heady pioneering days for black business. 'The National Union of Mine-workers [NUM] condemned me for wanting to take over old, useless mines.'

But Motsepe persisted, and it took five long years to get even close to what he wanted from Anglo American. The first step was to form a new mining venture, Future Mining, which would offer services to

Anglo American's Vaal Reefs gold mine on a contractual basis and generate cash flow for Motsepe's company.

Within three years, Motsepe had transformed Future Mining into African Rainbow Minerals Gold (ARM Gold) – the root of his current vast investments in mining. He managed to purchase the marginal shafts he'd wanted and went in search of others. The mining fraternity was baffled. What could Motsepe do with these loss-making shafts that Anglo American couldn't? Even Harry Oppenheimer, the chairman of Anglo American, allegedly once buttonholed Motsepe at a function and asked, 'What makes you think you are going to make money where Anglo has not?'

A lean management structure was at the top of Motsepe's list, plus a dash of innovation acquired in the days of sweeping gold dust in the mines.

'When Anglo closed down mines and retrenched 8 000 workers, we went to NUM [then the biggest mining union in the land] and said we'd take 6 000 people, pay them less, but they'll share in the profits. The workers agreed. If they didn't buy in, we would not be here [today].'

I have reported on mining unions for more than 10 years, and I can honestly say that a pay cut, no matter how constructive the reason, is an abhorrence to mine workers and can be resented for years. But in Motsepe's case, there were many who didn't agree.

Motsepe believes ARM Gold got it right in the boardroom, too.

'Anglo had high-grade mines,' Motsepe explained. 'Issues of efficiency are a bit of a luxury when you come from a culture of abundance. Running marginal mines is a humbling job – it is do or die.'

With this in mind, Motsepe cut overheads by foregoing an office in Johannesburg, a few hours' drive away, and worked out of a basic building in Orkney. He also changed the shift roster – another sensitive issue for workers. Shafts would be productive for 353 days a year, a substantial increase from 276 days. Nevertheless, the deal with the workers held, and within three years Motsepe had paid back the $8.2 million he had borrowed to make his dream a reality.

His next move was a canny boardroom reshuffle. Getting into bed with the major gold producer, Harmony, instead of competing with it, would prove a shrewd decision.

Motsepe explained how this came about. 'When Anglo was diversifying and didn't want to just be in South Africa, Bernard Swanepoel [the then CEO of Harmony] would better any offer I made. He was listed and had access to finance. I wasn't listed and I got finance expensively.'

When both men bid for a company called Freegold, Motsepe approached Swanepoel.

'I said, "The only company that benefits from us paying more is Anglo." We then merged ARM Gold with Harmony, went to Anglo and got a good deal [on Freegold].'

That merger has stood the test of time. In 2017, 14 years later, the joint venture between Harmony and ARM Gold is still going strong.

'My policy is: Hire the best and pay them well,' says Motsepe.

But all the smart hiring in the world may not ward off the biggest threat to mining in South Africa: nationalisation. Government, as well as some opposition parties, have mulled over the idea for years, even though it does not appear as if they have the will to take over one of the most lucrative industries in Africa. Julius Malema, leader of the ultra-left political party the Economic Freedom Fighters (EFF), would nationalise the mining industry tomorrow if he came to power, and the one million voters who cast their ballot for the EFF appear to support him in this.

Motsepe, however, prefers a mixed economy of world-class private businesses working side by side with a strong developmental state. But he does admit that business doesn't care about the welfare of the people as much as it does about dividends.

'When I confer with business colleagues, I recognise that there are things they don't understand. These are good people, mind you, but they were not brought up in a culture of having an obligation to listen to the poor. Our challenge is, how do we present an argument to our people so that they understand that this mixed economy we have now –

where there's a globally competitive private sector that coexists with a strong developmental state – is what we need?'

Motsepe practises what he preaches. In late 2011, he was in Modikwa, in northern Limpopo Province, to open a new $9-million road his company had built to connect 100 000 people living in remote villages to the national road. It had taken 14 months to construct and created thousands of jobs. Deputy President Kgalema Motlanthe gave the keynote address at the opening ceremony, and the ANC Youth League president at the time, Julius Malema, a son of Limpopo, was a special guest.

On that day, Motsepe said that ARM Gold had felt 'an obligation' to fund the project, despite the reservations of his New York–based shareholders, who believed that building roads was a government responsibility. Clearly, the New Yorkers spent little time living and working in Africa, where business and politics often intersect.

Overall, Motsepe believes that South Africa should be proud of its post-apartheid achievements, initiated in glorious fashion by Nelson Mandela. We should expect no less of the current leadership, Motsepe said, and in a meeting between business and government, he had made this clear to President Jacob Zuma. 'We have to be globally competitive and attractive in whatever we do,' he told the president.

Motsepe has vowed to give much of his wealth away to the people – not as handouts, but in the form of grants and bursaries to deserving cases. His people travel the length and breadth of the country to meet with potential candidates and assess applications.

When Motsepe announced this great giveaway in January 2013, he joked that he was already involved in charity because he owned a football club. Motsepe bought the yellow and green machine, Mamelodi Sundowns, in 2004. He had supported the team since he was a child in Mmakau. The villagers remember Motsepe as a talented young footballer who plied his trade with two teams around Mmakau, Magnificent FC and Dynamos FC, before his education overshadowed his promising football career.

When he wasn't playing, Motsepe went to watch Pretoria Sundowns – the forerunners of Mamelodi Sundowns – in the old Federation

Soccer League with fleet-footed players like Smiley Moosa and Vincent Julius. Football is Motsepe's passion, but it costs him millions of rands a year.

'We went into soccer not to make money, but as a means of giving back,' Motsepe explained. 'Of course, we never thought we would lose so much money! But it is important for people to know that they can relate to you, that you are not an arrogant, wealthy, aloof, uninvolved person.'

How does it feel to pour so much cash into a bottomless pit?

'It's okay,' Motsepe said with a shrug and a curl of his lip. 'People must see you as someone who is fallible, who also makes mistakes. I'm a sinner. I fumble. People must see me as one of them. Things that worry them must worry me. Other than being miserable watching Sundowns, I have very little else. I have one home and not even one holiday home. I fly around the world a lot, all the time, and I spend a lot of money doing it. I was resisting it, but I am going to have to get a private jet. It's unavoidable. The problem is, these things are expensive.'

In 2016, it was sun up rather than Sundowns ... The team rewarded Motsepe for his years of tears and investment of millions when they won both the Premier Soccer League in South Africa and the African championship. Motsepe even paid for 140 Sundowns fans to fly to Cairo for the second leg of the final, against Egyptian giants Zamalek.

And the paying didn't stop, even then. As his team finally raised the trophy above their heads and basked in the glory before tens of thousands of football fans, Motsepe told the players that the $1.5-million prize money, which was payable to the club, would be shared among them. How charitable is that?

17

A voyage of discovery

Adrian Gore

Adrian Gore

Adrian Gore is a dapper man, always impeccably turned out in a sharp suit with an open-neck shirt. In public, he is quiet and polite to a T. But underlying these characteristics is the professional drive that has allowed him to build and run a massive company. No wonder he is regarded as one of the best business leaders to have emerged from Africa in the past two decades.

Gore was born in Johannesburg in 1964 to two academics. He is a businessman who plays his cards close to his chest – his motto is 'Don't talk about it until you've done it' – and in business he sticks to what he knows best. Those who know Gore are not surprised when he says that the only investment he has is shares in his own company, one that he started building more than 24 years ago and has transformed into a global, diversified financial services group: Discovery Holdings, with an income of more than $4 billion a year.

Forget about the old investing adage of not putting all your eggs in one basket – Gore has. He owns about 9 per cent of the JSE-listed Discovery Holdings and has personal wealth of $480 million, according to *Forbes*.

The fact that Gore is invested to the hilt in his own company must make his shareholders sleep easier. It is a sign that Gore practises what he preaches in a business that is rarely far from his mind.

I once interviewed Gore in a TV studio for CNBC Africa. He asked me whether I was a Discovery member, and I said that I was. 'It's okay, you look healthy,' he said, and we both laughed. Discovery Holdings built its name on its Vitality programme, which rewards members for going to the gym, eating healthy food and getting regular medical check-ups.

Gore, who looks good for a man in his early 50s, especially considering the pressure he faces in the business world, regularly jogs the six kilometres to his office. He is a devout orthodox Jew who saves the Sabbath for family and contemplation. One of his few vices is drinking up to a dozen espressos a day.

'I'm up every morning at 4.30 a.m., training. I'm definitely a bit obsessive-compulsive when it comes to training. Everywhere I go, I run up and down the fire escapes. Even between appointments, I'm up and down the fire escapes,' Gore once told the *Mail & Guardian*. He recalled that he was in a hotel in Chicago once when it caught fire and he was the only guest who knew where the fire escapes were!

When Gore had his huge glass-and-steel headquarters built – it dominates West Street, the main road running through the Sandton business district – he had a running track put on top so that he and his staff can work out at lunch time. On a nice day, when Gore is on the track under a blue sky, he must feel a deep sense of satisfaction that he is running on top of South Africa's leading medical insurer, which provides health insurance for more than 200 000 companies and nearly two million people and has cornered half the market.

It is a lifetime away from the lean business beginnings of Discovery in 1991. On the day Gore left Liberty Life, where he was a young actuary, he was in his late 20s. He had the idea of starting up a small life insurance unit within financial services group FirstRand through an unbundling from the listed parent company. According to legend, he first offered the idea to his then boss, Liberty founder Sir Donald Gordon, who turned him down.

Gore then took the idea to Laurie Dippenaar, the father of First-Rand (and worth $610 million, according to *Forbes*). Nearly a quarter of a century later, Dippenaar still remembers vividly his first meeting with Gore.

'You could immediately see that this guy was different. He was not the typical chartered accountant, nerdy smart. You could see he had intelligence, but he also had business sense; all the qualities that make you a success. I think he is actually one of the smartest businesspeople I have ever met.'

According to Dippenaar, Gore's first pitch didn't go well. The life insurance scheme Gore set out was too much like the others, Dippenaar thought.

'To this day, he says I got it wrong. A year later he comes up and says he's got something completely different. From life insurance he had gone to health insurance. He started to describe what he had in mind, and I could immediately see that he was onto something.'

That something became Discovery.

'When he described the medical savings account, it was a pioneer move in South Africa,' Dippenaar recalls. 'I remembered when I was a bachelor and paying all these premiums for health insurance. You are young and healthy – you don't need to claim. All you do is pay premiums. Here was a product where you could carry forward some of the premiums if you were not claiming. In theory, you could get into a situation where you didn't have any premiums to pay.'

Gore left his job and Dippenaar lent him an office. He gave Gore three months to draw up a business plan.

'He never had any hesitation. He came up with the numbers. We liked it. So we backed him,' Dippenaar says.

The rest, as they say, is history. Gore has since forged ahead into overseas markets and made a fortune one country at a time. In China, Discovery has a 25 per cent stake in Ping An Health Insurance, the country's largest private health insurer. It does business with companies like Volvo, Unilever and Goldman Sachs.

Nick Crail, a portfolio manager at RMB Private Bank, says, 'China remains a huge growth market, with the estimated total healthcare spend expected to rise by over 90 per cent by 2020. Private healthcare spend is expected to grow even stronger over this period. Ping An has established itself as the leader in Critical Illness Insurance and related spend, a strong position to be in, given that approximately 65 per cent of deaths are classified as non-communicable diseases. By increasing their stake, Discovery has identified this opportunity.'

In Britain, where the competition is tough, the company has created the fourth largest insurer in an alliance with old stager Prudential. It also has ties to Humana Inc. in the United States, and the AIA Group in Singapore.

'Getting into these markets is brutal,' Gore says. 'There's no easy way or short cut. Each market takes time.'

The market appears to approve of the AIA deal in Singapore. On the day it was signed, Discovery shares shot up by 6.6 per cent.

Paul Theron, CEO of asset managers Vestact, says Gore's character has been key to Discovery's success. 'His growth has been amazing. It wasn't a completely unique product that he was selling, coming out of Investec to start Discovery. But to go from that tiny firm to span into a global expansion has been brilliant.

'They had some problems in the US. But in the UK they have been able to offer a good product around Vitality. The intellectual property is certainly something that will do well there.'

Gore is undoubtedly the darling of his shareholders, as well as share speculators, but that's not to say he is liked by all. He has his fair share of enemies and detractors. He stands accused, for example, of squeezing competitors out at every opportunity, a charge he denies vehemently.

'I don't think that is fair. We are strong competitors and more competition is good for society. We do nothing unfairly.'

It's not only competitors who are unhappy. Doctors have taken issue with Discovery's payment rates, where practitioners are forced to cap their rates and accept smaller fees.

Gore's defence? There's nothing wrong with that practice. 'After all, we are the paymaster.'

And what about the hundreds of thousands of people covered by Discovery Health? Some of them are of the opinion that Discovery is making huge profits on the back of above-inflation medical-rate increases, while bombarding them with peripheral benefits like gym contracts and discounted flights.

On the day that Gore announced Discovery's financial results, furious customers turned to a business-news website to complain bitterly about their shrinking benefits, while others used words like 'robbery', 'rip-off' and 'gimmick' to describe Vitality.

'These are natural issues,' Gore says calmly. 'They see the money we make.'

It doesn't seem to bother him much though, as history has proven that customers tend to stick with Discovery.

'The customer satisfaction rate is very high,' Gore says proudly. Honesty and optimism have been the watchwords at Discovery from the day it was established, says the man who, in his own words, prides himself on being innovative and prudent.

'Building insurance around making people healthy may be quite soppy,' he says, but it has brought success in international markets. 'We know where to be bold and when to be reticent. We are pushing hard on the ground, taking no prisoners. We are ruthless.'

Gore's steely, ruthless side is often compared to that of Apple founder Steve Jobs, who was loved and hated in equal measure. Perhaps tellingly, there are two framed pictures of Jobs in Gore's palatial office in Sandton. One is from a business-leadership article and the other features Jobs on the cover of *The Economist*. Gore is at pains to explain that Jobs graced that cover for an edition that carried a story about Discovery. In the piece, *The Economist* hails Discovery's Vitality programme as innovative and as an example of how quickly new ideas flow from emerging markets to take on the world.

As for Jobs, Gore finds him very inspiring – especially for his obsession with one product. Sound familiar?

'An obsession with a solution for society,' says Gore, who feels the same way about Discovery. 'Every organisation must be started by someone; the owner-manager culture has a certain drive to it, a certain authenticity.'

It is no surprise that Discovery leans heavily on the management team that helped found it – few have left in more than 20 years.

'But what's most exciting about Discovery is that the future is ahead of us,' Gore says.

That future, though, may be under threat as long as the South African government pushes ahead with its proposed National Health Insurance (NHI) scheme. In 2015, the government published a White

Paper in which it set out its intention to impose a compulsory medical scheme for all, funded by the taxpayer, which would reduce private healthcare schemes to providing what it calls 'merely complementary services'. South Africa's health minister, Aaron Motsoaledi, says it is going to be a marathon rather than a sprint to introduce the scheme, but the private healthcare industry is understandably nervous. Discovery, which makes most of its profit in South Africa, should be especially concerned.

Analysts believe that the government health scheme will make a huge dent in the profits of the medical insurance industry, big enough to send a few companies under. They single out Discovery as one company that is at risk, because of its high administration and care charges.

'We will have to adapt in some way, but I don't think it's threatening at all,' claims Gore.

While Gore calls NHI 'excellent and rational' and says that it could strengthen the public system dramatically, he claims that it won't supplant the country's private healthcare system and will take much longer to introduce than the 12 to 13 years the government has given itself.

If history is anything to go by, there can be no doubt that Gore and his team – often called the best brains in the industry – are busy preparing for the advent of NHI, which probably explains the company's involvement in at least one NHI pilot project.

'Status quo is undesirable,' Gore says. 'You can't have huge portions of the population with no access to proper healthcare. It's not good for the country. I don't think a great business exists on the back of dysfunctionality. You can't exist at the expense of society. You've got to be part of society.'

But what *is* he doing for society? That is, when he is not working or spending time with his family? Driven by his philosophy that only entrepreneurs create jobs, Gore chairs Endeavor South Africa, the local chapter of a global non-profit organisation that seeks to identify and nurture young entrepreneurial talent.

It's where he hopes to find, mentor and offer a break to future

Gores – perhaps in much the same way Dippenaar did for him 21 years ago.

The first lesson, surely, is don't talk about it until you've done it, and don't take any prisoners.

18

'I wanna be a billionaire – tonight!'

Abdulsamad Rabiu

Abdulsamad Rabiu

'I AM NOT VERY happy, you guys,' a gruff voice said over the telephone to Abisola Owolawi on a hot Lagos night. 'You have me down as a millionaire, but I am a billionaire – twice over!'

It was the voice of Abdulsamad Rabiu, one of the cement kings of Nigeria, speaking to the *Forbes Africa* correspondent for West Africa at the time. Clearly, Rabiu was upset and wanted recourse.

When Abisola, a young Nigerian journalist in her mid-20s, relayed the conversation to me in Johannesburg the next day, I uttered four words that set in motion a remarkable encounter with the secret wealth of one of Africa's richest people. 'Let him prove it,' I said. I looked at the current *Forbes* rich list and saw that Rabiu was down for a 'mere' $670 million.

In weeks of frantic research across London, Lagos, New York and Port Harcourt, *Forbes Africa* eventually uncovered the continent's newest billionaire. It may have taken gallons of midnight oil, plentiful late-night phone calls and loads of headaches, but it was an exhilarating discovery for anyone interested in global business. And it yielded a fascinating cover story for our November 2013 issue.

I am often asked how *Forbes* and *Forbes Africa* calculate a person's net worth. It is quite a process, I can tell you. It involves digging, checking and cross-checking. With African multimillionaires and billionaires, it often starts with our journalists in Johannesburg, Nairobi and Lagos, and ends with the *Forbes* wealth unit in the United States. The wealth unit acts as the auditors in the process to double-check and verify the work of the researchers. The United States crew are a bit like tax people – if they doubt a fact, they will not allow it. They always err on the side of caution.

The good news for those who dare to go through the process is that, at the end of it, they can get a solid-gold endorsement of their personal wealth with which few will argue.

How is it done? Well, most of the valuation is based on the value of the candidate's listed assets. Then it is up to the candidate to provide audited evidence of his or her assets, like private jets and properties. Bank accounts aren't of much use, even though – surprisingly – many candidates provide them. There is always the chance that money can be deposited into the account the day before the statement is submitted to *Forbes* and withdrawn the day after.

The wealth desk is always after a candidate's 'net worth'. So debts have to be tracked down, verified and then subtracted from the overall wealth figures.

The sad fact is that few of Africa's super-wealthy are prepared to go through this process. I suppose many fear the taxman, politicians or begging letters; whatever the reason, it often impedes *Forbes*'s mission.

So you can imagine the joy when Rabiu – who people say could be the next Aliko Dangote – offered his books up for scrutiny. Because Rabiu has been one of the big hitters in African business for many years. The publicity-shy chairman and CEO of BUA Group, a privately owned conglomerate dealing in cement, sugar and flour, with annual revenue estimated at $2 billion, has plans to invest $500 million in the country of his birth, Nigeria.

Forbes Africa's investigation into Rabiu's wealth unearthed a whole string of assets. BUA Group has interests in key sectors similar to those of Dangote. These include the above mentioned cement, sugar and flour, but through the group's subsidiaries, it also does business in real estate, steel, port concessions, manufacturing, oil, gas and shipping.

The group also owns the ship *BUA Cement 1*, a 200-metre-long vessel designed for heavy loads. It is Nigeria's first floating terminal.

In addition to his assets in the BUA Group, Rabiu owns property in Britain worth a staggering $62 million, and in South Africa worth $19 million. Among his properties is a house in Gloucester Square, London, worth nearly $16 million, with an Aston Martin and Bentley parked outside. He also has homes in Eaton Square and Avenue Road, two of the most expensive streets in Britain, known as Millionaires' Row. His neighbours include speculator George Soros and Chelsea FC owner Roman Abramovich. In Africa, he owns a $12.6-million penthouse at the One&Only in Cape Town, and he jets around the world in an eight-seater Gulfstream G550, powered by a Rolls-Royce BR710 turbofan engine and worth $44.9 million, as well as an $18-million Legacy 600 aircraft.

Rabiu's taste for the good life is evident.

After we had totted up all the shares and the aircraft and the properties, the next component we needed was Rabiu's debt, so that we could calculate his net worth. We sent Abisola to London to check out his assets there. In one of our late-night phone calls between Johannesburg and Lagos, I asked Rabiu whether he owed any money. He wasn't pleased with the question.

'I don't owe anyone anything! If anything, people owe *me* money,' he barked.

There were more calls, these to San Francisco, home of the head of the wealth unit Kerry Dolan. After long deliberations, the wealth unit finally revealed its findings to *Forbes Africa*: Rabiu's net worth was $1.2 billion.

Again, Rabiu was not happy.

'If anything, I am worth twice that,' was the late-night word from Lagos.

I told him there would be other assessments on other days, but the wealth unit would not do a recount. I eventually managed to placate Rabiu with my vision for the next cover: 'Africa's newest billionaire'. That he liked, and it brought to an end what was essentially a *Forbes* wealth-calculation case study.

Rabiu may have been born with a silver spoon in his mouth, but it was ripped away from him, by cruel circumstance, at a young age. His business career began when his businessman father was thrown into prison during a period of political turmoil in Nigeria. Rabiu was born in Nigeria's northern state of Kano. His father, Isyaku Rabiu, was a renowned businessman who had made a fortune in trade and industry in the decades after Nigeria's independence in 1960. By the 1970s, Isyaku's wealth and influence had grown considerably. He was a key sponsor of the National Party of Nigeria, which formed the government after the country returned to civilian rule following the elections of 1979.

But in 1983 the government was toppled in a military coup, which led to the arrest of the president, Shehu Shagari, and many of his close associates, including Isyaku.

Around this time, the young Rabiu earned his bachelor's degree in economics from Capital University in Columbus, Ohio, in the United States. He returned home to find his father's business in ruins following his incarceration. Barely 24 years old, with little experience of his own, Rabiu had to step in to save his father's business empire.

'It was very difficult,' remembers Rabiu. 'When we started, our dad was not there. There was this huge vacuum, because of his personality. He grew the business, he did everything, everybody reported to him, and then he wasn't there any more. So at a very tender age, I was saddled with so many things. I had to make a lot of important decisions, and don't forget that this happened suddenly.

'At the time, there were three ships being discharged – rice and sugar ships. The government agencies tried to seize the goods; so we were discharging, they were taking, we were taking back. It was a big, big issue. Those kinds of things were really challenging.

'The biggest challenge was that there were restrictions on confirming letters of credit because of the coup. Then there was the issue of the planes; there were two private jets and we didn't know what to do with them. We couldn't fly them. They actually grounded the jets. We were able to get the big one out and we decided we didn't need it. I just got rid of it.

'[My father] was in detention, so who was going to be flying a private jet at that time, with Major General Muhammadu Buhari [the former military dictator, and, ironically, the current elected president of the country] around? They grounded the small plane for two years, but it was returned after [my father] was released from detention.'

In 1988, Rabiu set up his own business, BUA International, with the blessing of his father, who by then had been released. He imported rice, sugar and edible oils, as well as iron and steel rods. His big break came in 1990, when a friend informed him of an opportunity to do a deal with a government-owned steel company.

Production at the Delta Steel Company had been severely hampered by the Nigerian government's decision to reduce grants. The company was considering approaching private business to finance the procurement of raw materials, and Rabiu saw an opportunity. But the deal needed government approval. After approaching the minister of steel, who hailed from Rabiu's home state, Rabiu was asked to finance the project.

'They only wanted three serious companies to participate, because they did not want to shut down Delta Steel. [The minister] went to the president and managed to get a special allocation to Delta Steel, but it wasn't enough. So, he asked if we would be able to get counter funding, and I said, "Of course." We approached First Bank, we showed them the proposal and they said they would need us to put in our equity.

'We were able to get the business, which was worth almost $20 million at the time, but the idea was that we were importing Delta Steel's raw materials to the tune of 25 000 to 30 000 tons per month, and instead of them paying us back in cash, they gave us the processed products. We didn't want to collect money, because at the time you would sometimes never get it.'

This payment method worked out favourably for Rabiu and his company, because the price of the products was government controlled. 'I think it was around $6.30 from the company, but around $90 in the open market. So it was quite a good opportunity for us, and we made quite a bit of money.'

By 1992, a regime change had come about and the honeymoon was over. With the substantial profits he had made from the steel venture, Rabiu invested in Tropic Commercial Bank, which operated in Nigeria. He became chairman of the bank after buying a majority shareholding.

In 1995, BUA acquired Nigeria Oil Mills, a peanut-processing company in Kano, for more than $20 million. The previous owners had offered BUA the business based on their status as a player in the edible-oils business. Two years later, BUA Flour Mills' first factory was established in Lagos. The Kano flour factory was launched in 1998. Thereafter, BUA set up its sugar refinery in Lagos. The 2 000 metric ton (MT) per day capacity plant is the second largest refinery in West Africa, after the Dangote Sugar Refinery, which produces an estimated 2 400MT per day.

It's a hot morning in Port Harcourt, which lies in the Niger Delta, when *Forbes Africa* visits one of Rabiu's biggest projects, BUA Mixed Development, which includes a sugar refinery with a production capacity of 2 000 tons per day and a 65 000MT storage, a flour mill, and a pasta, semolina and rice mill.

Engr Olumo, BUA Group's project coordinator in the eastern region, says of Rabiu: 'He is very analytical, balanced and always calm under stressful situations. In spite of being experienced, he is always willing to learn more.'

Rajan Sharma, the trade finance manager at Rabiu's equipment and material procurement company NOM UK adds, 'It has been wonderful seeing the company grow and prosper. Mr Rabiu is very approachable and reasonable. We have a team of 14 people working in the London office and we all feel as if we are a family. We are treated with the utmost respect. All employees approach Mr Rabiu on a first-name basis.'

Rabiu is often compared to Africa's richest man, Aliko Dangote, due to the fact that most of their businesses operate in the same sectors. Rabiu dismisses talk of any competition between them, pointing out that their mutual interests in certain sectors derive from the inclinations of the patriarchs of their respective families.

'We are both from Kano, and our parents were doing more or less the same kind of business, so we grew up in the trading environment. My dad had been doing rice, sugar and edible oil for a very long time. Aliko's grand-uncle, Sanusi Dantata, at one time was the biggest trader in terms of imports in Kano State,' he says. 'We've known each other since childhood. Although people seem to think that we are doing the sort of business that Aliko is doing, I keep telling them that this is a business that my family has been involved in before Aliko even started.'

BUA's sugar venture proved a cash cow. The company was able to reap huge margins because of the difference in duties for imports of raw sugar, which was 5 per cent, and that of finished, or white, sugar, which was 50 per cent. With the money he made from this business (he declines to reveal the exact amount), Rabiu cast his eye further afield. His research revealed that the cement business would offer good returns on investment. The first step was to secure a licence to import cement. Because of its scarcity, due to the fact that few companies held licences to import it, the price of cement was high. One of the conditions for obtaining a licence was that the candidate company should have a terminal where the raw cement could be processed and bagged. Another was that the candidate company should either own a plant in Nigeria, where production could take place, or be in the process of building one.

BUA set out to meet the requirements, starting with the acquisition of the Cement Company of Northern Nigeria (CCNN), which they bought from Scancem International for nearly $100 million in 2007. The next goal was to procure the terminal. Since it would have taken over a year to build one, Rabiu made a smart move and acquired a floating terminal. He approached the then president, Umaru Musa Yar'Adua, to obtain government approval. The terminal secured the import licence.

Production on this platform was carried out until last year, when the government restricted imports following the launch of Dangote's $1-billion cement plant in Ibese, Nigeria. Although Rabiu disagrees with the government's decision, he says he was prepared for it.

'When the Ibese plant was commissioned, the government decided that there was enough production capacity in Nigeria and there will be no need for imports. I still do not agree with that. We knew it was coming, so we decided to put up our own plant. Part of what we acquired from Scancem was a small grinding plant in Edo State, which is called Edo Cement, but then with a large limestone deposit. It is a 3-million-ton plant and costs a little over $500 million.

'At the same time, we are also looking at Ilaro, west Nigeria; in fact, I am going to China next week for a meeting with CDMI, a Chinese cement-plant manufacturer, to put up another plant in Ilaro. We want to capture part of the south-western market, because that is the biggest market in Nigeria today.'

Rabiu believes that Nigerian demand is greater than is currently estimated. He points out that when the additional supply is added and the price is adjusted further, latent demand will be unlocked.

'Nigeria has around 170 million people, and the production capacity that the country has is about 20 million, maybe 22 million tons. So that gives us about 117 kilograms per head. Nigeria is so low in relation to other African countries in terms of consumption per head. It has to go up, and I am looking at a minimum of 250 kilograms per head in the next three to four years. I think it will happen, and then we are looking at a minimum of 35 to 40 million tons' capacity.

'The price of cement in Nigeria is probably the highest anywhere in the world, apart from possibly Zambia, at $8.80 per bag, which is $173 per ton. It's around $40 per ton anywhere else in the world; why should it be $170? It doesn't make sense at all. Everybody says we have issues with infrastructure and power. It's nonsense. Power is cheap in Nigeria. Gas is cheap. We had to put up a power plant at Edo Cement, which is about $60 to $70 million. Capital expenditure is there, and it's quite a bit of money. But it costs you no more than $20 million a year for gas, and that is your biggest cost in a cement plant.'

Rabiu wants the price of products to decrease so that demand will increase. While cement has been a key focus of the group's activities in recent years, Rabiu is also eyeing the steel industry.

'In sub-Saharan Africa, Nigeria is the largest importer of steel and steel products, especially pipes, flat sheets and reinforcements, yet we do not have an integrated steel plant in the country.'

Plans are also being made to invest more in expanding the sugar business to exploit opportunities that have been created by the federal government's implementation of a national sugar master plan.

'We want to ensure that we have at least 30 000 hectares cultivated for sugar plantation in the next three years,' Rabiu explains. 'We have the Lafiaji sugar plantation, which we bought from the government around four years ago, but it is only around 15 000 hectares, so we are trying to develop another 30 000 hectares. We should be able to supply the entire region with sugar. We will look to take the West African market.'

For a man who can easily afford the best in life – he has a Bentley and Aston Martin parked in his courtyard – Rabiu's simplicity is remarkable. He speaks excitedly about going to see American jazz singer Stacey Kent whenever she performs in London. He is also a movie buff and always on the lookout for new releases. With a whiff of triumph, he declares that he just saw the biographical drama *Diana* before most people, which captures the last two years of the life of the Princess of Wales.

Rabiu exudes an aura of fulfilment. He gives the impression of someone who values his achievements and success, but he doesn't gloat about it. He may have been born with a silver spoon in his mouth, but Rabiu – Africa's newest billionaire – managed to carve out his own golden niche in the continent's business history all by himself.

Epilogue

Days of demons and angry elephants

No BOOK ON *Forbes Africa* and its billionaires would be complete without the story behind the story.

When you flick through the pages of the magazine, the relaxed poses in the glossy photographs make the process look like smooth sailing.

Think again. When I page through an issue, I am reminded of the image of the serene swan gliding smoothly down the river like a stately galleon. But what you don't see are the swan's legs paddling away frantically beneath the water ...

Working at *Forbes Africa* is a bit like that.

Life in Africa is never boring, as I found out when I flew to Mauritius in 2014 for a speaking engagement at an investment conference that had been arranged by the island's Board of Investment at one of its balmy coastal resorts. The island knows how to sell itself to the outside world; its immigration arrival cards are printed on bond paper, unlike the flimsy flyaway bits of paper you get in many African airports. You could frame them, put them up on the wall and pass them off as qualifications. When I touched down, a chauffeur-driven Porsche picked me up at the aircraft's steps and whisked me through a VIP lounge without the trouble of having to stand in a passport queue. My luggage was delivered to me.

Already I didn't need much persuasion to visit. Mauritius is a great story for a business journalist: how a sleepy, sugar-cane-growing, colonial island – a mere stop-off on the shipping routes between Cape Town and India – became a prosperous, high-tech Indian Ocean tiger.

When I landed in the capital of Port Louis, the World Economic

Forum (WEF) had just ranked Mauritius as the 45th most competitive economy in Africa. South Africa was 54th. It drew comparisons with another tiger – Singapore.

'The only difference between Singapore and Mauritius is that they had oil and we had sugar,' Ashok Kumar Aubeeluck, the head of economic research at the Bank of Mauritius, told me with a smile.

On the ground, I found that those not-so-sweet sugar days were almost over. Thirty years ago, 65 000 Mauritians worked in the sugar-cane fields, and sugar production made up nearly a third of the economy. These days, that number has dropped to around 14 000, with sugar making up a mere 1.2 per cent of the economy, according to Aubeeluck.

I could not have been more comfortable on my first night in paradise. A warm wind drifted in off the Indian Ocean and my eyes lolled drowsily like the palms on the beach of Turtle Bay a few yards from my hotel window. A quick dip in the huge egg-shaped bath in my room and my night would be complete; then I could rest ahead of my demanding speaking engagement the next day ... or so I thought.

Disaster. As I stepped out of the bath, my foot inside the tub slipped. The egg-shaped bath acted like a ski jump and my body went flying through the air. The last image I had, before I crashed down in agony, was of my right foot framed against the ceiling. My rib cage smashed, from a great height, into the sharp edge of the bath. I was bent double in agony, hardly able to breathe. In an instant I felt vulnerable and lonely. In 33 years of journalism, I had survived bricks, batons, tear gas and landmines, and here I was, done in by the sharp edge of a bath in paradise. This is it: Sod's law, I thought.

When I finally managed to straighten up, there was a huge red welt on my ribs. I elected not to be a boy and to just grin and bear it. I couldn't have slept anyway, so I phoned reception for a doctor.

'Fifteen minutes,' the doctor said.

'Oh yeah?' I thought.

But sure enough, a doctor in a white coat arrived at my door with a nurse, and on the dot, too. They strapped me into an ambulance to take me to hospital. It was dark and I didn't have a clue where I was going as the ambulance bounced along some of the rougher roads of Mauritius. I winced as I looked at my watch: six hours to go until my speaking date.

The hospital was strange; it appeared to be a converted boathouse, right on the edge of the ocean. A doctor treated me to the sounds of gently lapping waves a few yards away. Good treatment it was, too. The staff worked with professional ease and soon had me sorted out. They insisted that I remain overnight. So four hours after I'd landed in the country, I was lying in a hospital bed – heaven knows where – with a drip in my arm. I didn't know whether to laugh or cry. I chose to laugh.

The next morning, I had to argue for my release. Another bumpy ride back to the hotel, and I became surely one of the few conference speakers in history to arrive at a venue in an ambulance. I don't know how I managed to stand up and speak, in agony and full of painkillers, but I did and no one in the audience was any the wiser. They did, however, probably notice how I shied away from pats on the back and bear hugs afterwards.

Over the next two days I was back and forth between the hotel and the hospital, Clinique Du Nord in Tombeau Bay, with the help of the conference organisers. Scans showed that thankfully there were no broken ribs or a ruptured spleen, but I had a bruise on my side the size of Namibia. Best of all, I had health insurance from former *Forbes Africa* cover boy Adrian Gore that worked like a charm.

Throughout, I was impressed by the professional way in which the Mauritian doctors carried out their duties. Mauritius has more doctors per thousand people than most other nations, and it dreams of breaking into the health-insurance tourism industry, where people pay for first-class medical care in a luxury ward, followed by recuperation in a luxury hotel. India and South Africa are firmly ensconced in this business, catering to the wealthy who want cheaper operations and better weather in which to recuperate.

One of the proponents of the lucrative trade in repairing the knees and replacing the hips of the rich is Moussa Rawat, the chairman of Bramer Holdings, a company with $1.5 billion in assets. He is one of the richest men on the island and the scion of the wealthy Rawat family. He is also the nephew of the head of the family, the billionaire Hassam Moussa Rawat.

Moussa Rawat studied civil engineering at Edinburgh University and returned home to build a hospital, a dam and 360 kilometres of road. He claims that if Mauritius seriously invested in health tourism, it could take $200 million of business away from India alone.

'I think if we can get enough business, India will bring their doctors and hospitals here,' he says.

Many hard business heads in Port Louis agree that health tourism could be the golden goose for Mauritius. Almost all say that the biggest drawback is the island's isolation, which requires at least a three-hour flight from anywhere.

'We've got the doctors, we've got the hospitals. We need investment in more flights to connect us to the rest of the world. It is as simple as that,' says Rawat.

So that was my Mauritian adventure. After having done two tours of Angola during the civil war, having been beaten up, gassed, locked up and stun-grenaded in the 20 years that I have travelled the nooks and crannies of this continent, I attend a conference in paradise and am nearly permanently incapacitated. Oh, the irony!

But if there is anyone who can honestly claim that they are the Indiana Jones of *Forbes Africa*, it is Jay Caboz.

'I haven't got the hat,' says Jay when I mention it to him.

It says a lot about this hard-working journalist, who was turned down by two major newspapers before he applied to us for an internship. I thought he was a little odd – in an eccentric way – when I interviewed him for the job, but, as the years wore on, I thought it even odder that others had ignored his talents. Jay's meticulous attention to detail has won him a string of awards – a great return for a journalist only in his late 20s.

In short, give Jay a camera and he will go anywhere. Take the story with which he won the Standard Bank Young Journalist of the Year Award: about rats being trained to sniff out landmines in Angola. We all laughed when he told us the story, but it turned out to be true – rats were helping to clear villages in Angola from the curse of landmines laid in the country's civil war; one of the great tailpieces to what has been a terrible African tragedy.

On the weekend before Jay was to fly to Angola for the story, he dislocated his shoulder playing hockey. Undeterred, and without telling me – because I would have said no – Jay walked through the landmine fields with his one arm in a sling and a camera in the other. In fact, he walked through those fields for days without the use of one arm, often lying on the ground to take his award-winning shots.

When Jay found the story of the landlocked family Robinson, who hailed from the mining town of Carletonville near Johannesburg and were going to compete in the 5 500-kilometre Cape to Rio yacht race, he hitched a lift when they sailed their vessel from Port Elizabeth to Cape Town for the start of the race. Mike and Gill Robinson were going to race to Brazil with their sons Ricky, 23, Brennan, 22, and Ryan, 14; daughters Kathryn, 25, and Michaela, 10; and their nephew Bradley, 19, in the yacht *Ciao Bella*.

Soon after casting off from Port Elizabeth, Jay and *Ciao Bella* ran into the eye of a storm.

'The might of the Atlantic slams against the yacht in the inky blackness in the early hours of the morning. The inch-wide fibreglass hull shudders. It's too much for Andries Swart, a solid-built man wearing a red headlamp, who is thrown around like a ragdoll down the deck. He recovers and with the help of his headlamp he makes coffee. He hums to himself and says you would never expect him to be on a 32-foot yacht, rocking and sliding to two-metre swells at 2 a.m. somewhere off the coast of Mossel Bay,' read Jay's dispatch.

'"Brace, brace!" screams someone from above. With the headlamp illuminating the stove, Swart is thrown forward and backward by the power of the swell. He trips over the engine box and flips almost

360 degrees and slams against the chart table. Sea water gushes into the cabin as Swart lies face-down on the floor, soaked.

"'I think I've cracked a rib,' he groans.'

Jay made it back to dry land safe and sound and the family gave a good showing in the race.

In the same year, in the Lower Zambezi National Park in Zambia, Jay risked his neck again when he took to the Zambezi River in a bobbing canoe along with game ranger Wallace Kabompa, who grew up in the area.

"'The dangers are very real,' says Kabompa. "I have seen it first hand. When I was very young, I went swimming in a pool close to the river. I was swimming with my friend. What I saw, my friend went down, underwater, and then he went for good. I never saw him again. His parents came to me and said, "Where is your friend?" I said I didn't know. He had been eaten by a crocodile. I tell you, I have been beaten by my parents not to swim in the Zambezi. My parents would say, "Don't you know there are crocodiles; it's dangerous."'

As the sun was going down, Jay spotted a herd of elephants and asked Kabompa to paddle nearer so that he could take a shot.

Jay takes up the story: 'The elephants begin to cross the river, but as they reach our side of the shore, there's a problem. They get stuck. They panic, bodies crashing against one another. Their ears flap madly and they run into each other. They turn. They come straight for us. You may think an elephant charging in water is slow. Think again. An elephant slices through water like it's going through a field of grass. White water churns at their feet. Their trumpeting gets louder with every step. Their trunks smash the water. It is terrifying. When it's 50 metres away, you think it can never reach you. When it is 35 metres away, you worry that it will. When it's 15 metres, you realise one stamp of the foot could turn your body to dog meat.'

Kabompa, paddle in hand at the front of the canoe, came to the rescue.

Jay continues: 'He slams his paddle in the water violently, sending us in reverse paddle. Ten metres from us, where our canoe was a few moments before, the beasts take a sharp right-turn and scramble up the bank. I thank the heavens.

'"Was that close enough?" says Kabompa with a smile as wide as the Zambezi.'

Forbes Africa used the split-second image of a raging elephant that Jay had captured over a double page, and it was one of our pictures and narrow escapes of the year.

Fellow *Forbes Africa* photojournalist Motlabana Monnakgotla probably thought he would be safe when he went to cover a gathering of Christians in Pretoria. The focus of the article was an evangelical preacher from Zimbabwe, Walter Magaya, who had founded Prophetic, Healing and Deliverance Ministries. In this cash-for-prayers-answered game, people have coughed up millions to the 'church', which fronts a $10-billion investment company.

'Prophets of Profit in the Business of Belief' was the title of this piece on the business of religion, which was to win *Forbes Africa* journalist Ancillar Mangena Sanlam and CNN awards.

Motlabana is a slight, wiry man from Soweto and the sort of individual you would want fighting next to you in a trench if there was a war. He is quiet but reliable, a man in his 20s with a passion for his job. No matter how difficult the story or where you may send him, he will wave goodbye to the newsroom, sling on his backpack and get on with the job.

On this night, Magaya, who claims that over 200 000 worshippers attend his churches in Zimbabwe every weekend, drew thousands to his prayer session at the Pretoria Showgrounds.

At one point during the evening's proceedings, worshippers started flocking to the stage, claiming they were possessed by demons and needed divine help. Motlabana stood nearby, clicking away with his camera.

'Suddenly, like a rugby tackle, I felt someone grab me around my thighs; it was a woman,' Motlabana says. 'She grabbed me, lifted me, and the next thing I was on the ground, fighting. My one hand was in the air to protect my camera and the other was pushing her away to protect the sensitive parts of my body. She was mumbling loudly and crying.'

It took three large and very strong ushers to prise the woman off his body. All around him, people were throwing themselves on the ground, crying and vomiting in religious fervour.

'I got up and ran away from the demon zone to where I was seated, and checked for vomit. I was clean, but I felt dirty nonetheless. An usher who saw the attack ran to me and asked if I was okay. I was fine, but I looked back and thought, "What the eff did I just go through?"'

Motlabana resolved to wear work boots and a helmet to the next religious gathering he might have to cover. In that dry newsroom way he has of dealing with trauma, he says: 'If I could have hit her with my camera, I would have.'

It doesn't matter what stands in the way of *Forbes Africa* journalists, we will always make it through: demons, ocean squalls, elephants ... we take on all comers. That is what makes this magazine what it is. In Africa, we have only just started, but rest assured that our journalists – like our entrepreneurs – will be out there striving for those stories that reflect what promises to be a remarkable century for business in Africa.